Collecting Antique Pewter

What to Look For and What to Avoid

This book is dedicated
in memory of
John Carl Thomas

Collecting Antique Pewter
What to Look For and What to Avoid

The PEWTER COLLECTORS' CLUB of AMERICA INC.

Collecting Antique Pewter

What to Look For and What to Avoid

ISBN-13: 978-0-9787256-0-0
ISBN-10: 0-9787256-0-3

Published by The Pewter Collectors' Club of America

Authored by Wayne A. Hilt, Dr. Barbara J. Horan, William R. Snow and Mark C. Anderson

Edited by Barbara and Robert Horan, Phyllis and Wayne Hilt, Debra and Mark Brewitt, Christie and William Snow

Descriptive text for the sections covering Fakes, Forgeries & Reproductions was edited from recorded transcripts by John Carl Thomas with additional text written by Wayne A. Hilt

Primary Photography by William R. Snow

Other Photography by Wayne A. Hilt, Dr. Donald M. Herr, Robert Horan, Dr. Stanley Mueller, Quincy J. Scarborough, Robert Werowinski and Dr. Melvyn D. Wolf

Special Photography by Penny Leveritt, Historic Deerfield, Massachusetts

Designed by William R. Snow

Printed and bound by CS Graphics Pte Ltd., Singapore

Contents

John Carl Thomas

Foreword

On April 30, 1999, during the spring national meeting, it was unanimously decided by the Board of Governors of the Pewter Collectors' Club of America (PCCA) to utilize the John Carl Thomas Memorial Fund for the express purpose of writing a book on collecting pewter to include the nemesis of all collectors, fakes and forgeries.

John had long been active in the club as the resident scholar, and as put by one of the board members, "the consummate connoisseur". This is evidenced by the legacy of quality pieces that reside in collections, both public and private, throughout the country, placed there by Mr. Thomas. John also strove to preserve pewter in a manner that removed the signs of abuse while retaining the signs of age and normal wear and tear. A clean and lustrous surface enhances the lines created by the early craftsmen and craftswomen.

During John's tenure with the club he took on the chairmanship of the authenticity committee with a mandate from the club to acquire as many study pieces as he felt necessary to aid students of antique pewter in their endeavors to avoid the pitfalls of fakes and forgeries. Under his watch, many important examples of spurious pieces were acquired and catalogued.

Collectors have long known that fakes and forgeries have existed. There was, however, a period of time when discussion of the topic was taboo. In the Pewter Collectors' Club's infancy, members of the club were reluctant to discuss this topic openly. If a bad item showed up at a meeting, it was conveniently overlooked in order to avoid embarrassment for all.

Fortunately, as a club we have grown to know that we are all susceptible to making mistakes, being victimized, or wishing upon a gilded lily. The price of education is expensive as anyone who has had a child in an institution of higher learning or who pays local school taxes knows. So too the price of ignorance can be more expensive if someone wastes hard-earned funds on spurious pieces. Most collectors want to know if the item they have is good or bad so as to avoid similar mistakes in the future.

The PCCA believes a volume on this topic will encourage rather than discourage collectors. It will also let fakers know that they will be exposed. The Pewter Collectors' Club of America encourages all pewter collectors and pewter scholars to seek out additional information about newly discovered fakes and forgeries and share this information with others. This will ensure that future generations have the knowledge to become discriminating and satisfied collectors.

For the Pewter Collectors' Club of America,

Wayne A. Hilt
Authenticity Chairman

Acknowledgments

To assemble and publish a book of this nature requires a great deal of time and cooperation. Because all of the work has been voluntary, this volume was over seven years in the making. The Pewter Collectors' Club of America (PCCA) wishes to acknowledge the many individuals, both members and non-members, who contributed to this worthy effort.

Many thanks to the following members who provided pewter, or marks on pewter, from their personal collections for illustration in the chapter on *Collecting & Connoisseurship*:

Mark C. Anderson

Richard and Totney Benson

Mark P. and Debra H. Brewitt

Dr. Donald M. and Patricia T. Herr

Joel and Henrietta Hillman

Wayne A. and Phyllis Hilt

Robert and Dr. Barbara J. Horan

David M. Kilroy

Julia B. and Dr. Stanley Mueller

J. Garland and Frances Pass

Stanley B. and Rose Rich

John A. and Beth Schneider

William R. and Christie F. Snow

Charles V. Swain

Dr. Melvyn D. and Bette Wolf

George W., Jr. and Janice Wolfe

The club also extends its gratitude to members Dr. Donald Herr, Wayne Hilt, Charles "Bud" Swain and Dr. Melvyn Wolf for providing many of the legitimate touchmarks appearing in the chapter on *Fakes, Forgeries & Reproductions*.

The PCCA Study Collection of fakes, forgeries and reproductions was assembled over many years. While the number of individuals who donated pieces to this collection are too numerous to list here, the club wishes to thank all of those people, both past and present, who have helped build this valuable resource.

Photographing all of the pewter, pewter marks (correct and incorrect) and other objects illustrated in the book was a laborious process. Most of this photography was done by William Snow and the club greatly appreciates his efforts. Other members who supplied photographs for this publication include Wayne Hilt, Dr. Donald Herr, Robert Horan, Dr. Stanley Mueller, Stanley Rich, Quincy J. Scarborough, Robert Werowinski and Dr. Melvyn Wolf. In addition, members who provided items other than pewter to be photographed are Richard C. Graver, Wendell Hilt, and A. Buol Hinman.

The club also thanks PCCA members and Master Pewterers Richard Graver and Jonathan Gibson for their help. A special thanks goes to Past President Richard Graver who specifically opened his workshop for two day-long photo sessions. Photos from Mr. Graver's workshop and Mr. Gibson's workshop appear in the chapter on *Construction & Fabrication*.

The photograph for the dust cover to this book was taken in the 18th century home of PCCA member Glenn Hillman. The club thanks him for opening his wonderful house expressly to obtain this image.

The exacting task of creating the Index for this volume was performed by PCCA member Debra Brewitt. The club and the John Carl Thomas Memorial Book Committee wishes to extend their gratitude for this time consuming work.

Other PCCA members who contributed to the effort to publish this volume are Past President Thomas A. Madsen, who has overseen the management of the John Carl Thomas Memorial Fund, and current PCCA Treasurer, Terry J. Ashley. The club would also like to thank all those members who have generously contributed to the John Carl Thomas Memorial Fund. Proceeds from that fund have been used to offset publishing costs.

The PCCA would like to recognize other individuals, outside of the organization, who had a hand in helping the club with this book. The club owes a particular debt of gratitude to Amanda Lange, Curator of Historic Interiors, and Penny Leveritt, Photographer, at Historic Deerfield in Deerfield, Massachusetts. Thanks to Ms. Lange, Ms. Leveritt provided several important photos of pewter making tools once used by Samuel Pierce of Greenfield, Massachusetts, and now in the permanent collection at Historic Deerfield.

In addition, the club extends its thanks to the staff of Old Salem in Winston-Salem, North Carolina. Photos of Master Pewterer Earl Williams and the Old Salem pewter workshop appear in the chapter on *Construction & Fabrication*.

Other non-member assistance was provided by Mr. William Bartley (crowned X die), Ms. Noelle Bikoff (photo retouching), and Mr. Thomas F. Lord (wood brace for the porringer handle casting photo).

The club also thanks John D. Davis, PCCA Honorary Member and Senior Curator of Metals at Colonial Williamsburg, Donald L. Fennimore, Curator Emeritus of Metals at Winterthur Museum, Susan Randolph, Director of Communications at Winterthur Museum, and Joseph Roundtree, Director of Publications at The Colonial Williamsburg Foundation for their valuable advice in the publication of this volume.

Finally, the PCCA wishes to express much gratitude to the John Carl Thomas Memorial Book Committee: Mark C. Anderson, Wayne A. Hilt, Robert and Barbara Jean Horan, and William R. Snow. The considerable time and talents of these members have helped make this book a reality. In particular, the club thanks Robert and Barbara Horan. Their insight and efforts to record comments on the PCCA Study Collection by John Carl Thomas before his death were the primary catalysts for the publication of this ground-breaking volume.

Introduction

Collecting antique pewter, like collecting antiques in general, can be fun, exciting and intellectually stimulating. However, becoming a serious collector requires knowledge. The more a collector knows about antique pewter, the more critical and discerning the collector becomes.

The purpose of this book is to help educate present and future collectors of antique pewter. To achieve that end, the authors of this volume have chosen to focus on an aspect of collecting that previous publications have only touched on: "Fakes, Forgeries and Reproductions". Selected pieces from the Pewter Collectors' Club of America (PCCA) Study Collection provide readers with an in-depth review of this topic. By reading and examining the pieces illustrated from that collection, the collector will be better able to identify and avoid items that are not legitimate antiques.

Two additional aspects of collecting will also be presented. 1. "Collecting and Connoisseurship" details the positive aspects of collecting by illustrating various criteria used to evaluate and distinguish period pewter. 2. "Construction and Fabrication" reviews the methods and materials used to create the many forms of antique pewter produced throughout history.

Before beginning the specifics of collecting, it would be beneficial to briefly review the history of pewter and pewter collecting.

Pewter was first used to manufacture vessels by the Egyptians, Romans, and other ancient civilizations. In Europe, pewter was utilized extensively from medieval times to the end of the 18th century. After that period, pottery and porcelain began to replace pewter as the materials of choice for serving food and drink.

Pewter was also used and manufactured in North America, from the Colonial period to the 1860s. In the beginning, English export wares made up the vast majority of pewter objects in use at the time. A ban on the export of block tin, the primary ingredient in pewter, made it difficult for American makers to compete. Up until the American Revolution, they were forced to rely on recycled pewter for their wares. After that time, additional sources of block tin became available.

Despite this early problem, a number of regional centers for manufacturing pewter emerged. These included various locations in New England, as well as New York and Pennsylvania. Later, pewter making expanded as far south as Georgia and as far west as Ohio. Today, while much of the antique pewter found in the U.S. originated in England, a great deal of American pewter still survives.

Collecting pewter in the U.S. actually began during the second half of the 19th century. One of the first individuals to collect "old wares" was Solon L. Newton of Greenfield, Massachusetts. Mr. Newton purchased his first piece of pewter, a pitcher, in May of 1872.[1] Over the next 29 years, he purchased over 200 additional pieces of pewter.[1] That collection, along with other antiques, was bequeathed to the Pocumtuck Valley Memorial Association in 1901 and is on view today in Deerfield, Massachusetts.[2]

By the early 20th century, interest in collecting pewter began to grow. In 1924, J.B. Kerfoot published *American Pewter*, the first comprehensive look at pewter made in America. While fraught with inaccuracies, Kerfoot provided a solid foundation for subsequent scholars.

A few years later, Howard H. Cotterell authored *Old Pewter, Its Makers and Marks*. Issued in 1929, this ground-breaking volume was the first in-depth listing of English manufacturers and their marks. Re-published in 1963, this book is still considered one of the best sources for identifying touchmarks on English pewter.

In 1940, Ledlie I. Laughlin published *Pewter in America, Its Makers and Their Marks*, the first two of three volumes, which became the definitive study of American pewterers. The third volume, which updated and added to the originals, was published in 1971.

Over the years, other books on American and English pewter have been written. Carl Jacobs published *Guide to American Pewter* in 1957, Christopher Peal penned *British Pewter & Britannia Metal* in 1971, Charles Montgomery offered *A History of American Pewter* in 1973, and John Carl Thomas, to whom this book is dedicated, wrote *Connecticut Pewter and Pewterers* in 1976. These volumes, and many others listed in the Bibliography, have added significantly to our knowledge of antique pewter.

Two other important catalysts for pewter collecting were the founding of The Pewter Society in England in 1918, followed by the founding of the Pewter Collectors' Club of America in 1934.

The first gathering of what was to become the Pewter Collectors' Club of America took place on March 21, 1934 at the Old State House in Boston.[3] This meeting, organized by then antiques editor of the *Boston Evening Transcript* William G. Dooley, brought together approximately 30 individuals with a common interest in pewter.[4] A governing body was chosen and on April 4th of that same year, the PCCA was formally established.[3] Today, the PCCA numbers over 600 memberships worldwide and its official semi-annual scholarly publication, *The Bulletin*, has been issued continuously since the club was founded.

This book, assembled and published by the PCCA in memory of John Carl Thomas, offers new and important information to the world of pewter collecting. The PCCA hopes it will greatly benefit current and future generations of pewter collectors.

References

1. McGowan, Susan. *Solon L. Newton Pewter Collection*. Deerfield, Mass: Pocumtuck Valley Memorial Association, 1998, p. 8.

2. McGowan, *Solon L. Newton Pewter Collection*, p. 2.

3. Perkins, Elisabeth M. "Recollections of the First P.C.C.A. Meeting". *The Bulletin*, PCCA, Vol. 6, No. 1, p. 5-6.

4. *Pewter in American Life*: Thomas, John Carl, ed. Pewter Collectors' Club of America. Providence, RI: Mowbray Company, 1984, p. 10.

Collecting

& Connoisseurship

Collecting & Connoisseurship

Collecting is a very personal pursuit and collecting pewter is no exception. Pewter is collected to satisfy many different interests. Some collect flatware: e.g. plates, dishes and chargers. Others prefer hollowware used for consuming beverages such as tankards, mugs and beakers. Some individuals collect only 18th century objects while others like a broad historical representation.

But no matter one's personal preference, the key to developing an interesting and valued collection of pewter is twofold. The first is the act of collecting itself. To collect means to gather together, to assemble. The second is developing the expertise necessary to achieve a desired result. This expertise is often referred to as connoisseurship. Connoisseurship is defined as having expert knowledge and a keen sense of discrimination in a particular field.

Becoming a connoisseur of antique pewter takes considerable time and requires a strong desire to learn. This chapter will assist the collector in that effort by illustrating several important aspects of antique pewter. Each of these aspects plays a significant role in helping to make decisions about how and what to collect.

Form is defined as the shape of an object, the proportion of its parts and how these parts work in conjunction with one another.

Style refers to the distinctive visual features of an object. These features can be used to help determine when and where an object was made.

Period is the interval in history in which a particular object was created. Shape, size, and method of construction are key factors in determining period.

Rarity refers to the overall availability of objects. If only a few examples of a particular object are known, it is considered rare. Rarity usually relates directly to value.

Function is defined as the purpose for which an object was made. Most pewter was made for purely utilitarian reasons and some items were multi-purpose. However, the designs used by pewterers quite often reflected the importance of a pleasing form.

Condition is the state of appearance in which an object presently exists. While a certain amount of wear on antique pewter may be expected, serious blemishing and extensive damage adversely affects desirability and value.

Marks are the identifying impressions applied to pewter. Knowledge of the many marks found on pewter helps the collector determine the maker of an object, where it was made, when it was made, the quality of the materials used, and whether or not an object met certain standards of measure. *Primary marks* are those placed by the pewterer identifying the object as his product. *Secondary marks* are placed by the pewterer or others and include, but are not limited to, city marks, house marks, quality marks, marks of verification, and owner's initials. Understanding marks also plays a very important role in helping to identify fakes, forgeries, and reproductions.

Decoration refers to ornamentation which was applied to some antique pewter. Decoration can be as simple as a manufacturing technique used to embellish an object or as complex as hand-engraved religious symbols, or a scene of historical significance.

Attribution is the ability to identify the maker of an object when no mark(s) exist. Form, size, style and understanding the use of interchangeable parts all contribute to attribution.

In addition to these aspects, other features of collecting pewter one should consider are color, provenance and materials. While pewter may appear dull gray at first, true antique pewter has a soft, reflective luster that distinguishes it from silver and other bright metals. Provenance refers to the history of ownership of a particular object. Provenance helps to determine legitimacy and often adds significantly to an object's value. Materials will be discussed in the following chapter on *Construction & Fabrication*.

Handling antique pewter is also an important step in the learning process. A collector develops a "feel" for the metal by examining many different objects, sensing their color, weight, and quality.

Restoration plays an important role in collecting antique pewter as well. Restoration is the exacting and expert repair to damage on a piece of pewter. Unlike many other antiques, quality restoration of pewter usually enhances its value. In some extreme cases, extensive restoration such as the replacement of a missing lid or handle is totally acceptable, especially when an object is of significant rarity. There are many makers who are represented by just a few surviving objects, thus making the conservation of these objects a "must".

Last, but not least, collectors of pewter are urged to read the many volumes that have been published on the subject over the years. The more knowledge one has about this fascinating subject, the more adept one becomes in the collecting process. The Bibliography found at the back of this volume will assist in that process. It is also important to remember that as time passes research moves forward, changing some previously-held opinions and attributions. Serious collectors need to recognize and accept this reality.

Form

Recognizing the subtleties of form is an important step to becoming a knowledgeable collector.

The two pieces of hollowware illustrated on these pages are classic examples of the best in 18th century form.

The English Queen Anne style teapot below by John Townsend demonstrates how size, proportion and balance come together to present a visually appealing whole. Note how the individual elements (i.e. body, lid, handle, spout and finial) work as one. No single part seems dominant or out of place with the other.

Form

This American chalice by New York pewterer Peter Young shows how proportion and balance work in tandem to produce a form that is both useful and elegant. Tall, late 18th century American chalices display a structure and symmetry almost without rival in pewter made during that period.

Form

Saucers, plates, dishes, chargers and basins comprise a grouping of forms called flatware. These forms were sometimes referred to as sadware in the 17th and 18th centuries. Size and depth usually determined how each item was categorized.

Basins, such as the marked American example to the right, were bowls with a narrow rim and generally ranged in size from 6 to 12 inches in diameter. There were some 14 inch basins made.

Saucers were generally smaller than 5 inches in diameter while plates ranged in size from 5 inches to 10 inches. Dishes were 10 inches in diameter and larger. Large English dishes, 18 inches in diameter and over, are often referred to as Chargers. Oval dishes, or platters, were made in several sizes.

Form

Pictured on this page are classic examples of 19th century American hollowware.

As both coffee and tea became more plentiful, serving vessels grew larger. The tall coffeepot to the right by Massachsetts pewterer Israel Trask is often referred to as a "lighthouse" style because of its distinctive shape.

The oval teapot below with the engraved eagle is also by Israel Trask. Later in the Federal Period one begins to see true "tea sets" which included a sugar bowl, creamer, a slop or waste bowl, and occasionally, a trivet.

Again, shape, balance, proportion, utility and overall appearance help to define outstanding form.

Style

Regional preferences play a key role in defining style. The hollowware pictured on these two pages helps to illustrate those regional differences.

The solid or "strap-handle" quart mug to the left is a style only found in the Boston or Rhode Island area, while the mug directly below, with its high fillet, is a style most often associated with New York.

The tulip-shaped mug at the bottom left was popular in and around Philadelphia. This one is by William Will. Many mugs and tankards of this style were also exported to New England and the Mid-Atlantic region from England.

There are some exceptions to these regional styles, but knowing the differences in design can often help identify an unmarked piece.

Style

The unmarked tankard to the right, with its spired lid and elongated thumb-rest, was a style popular around Boston.

The flat lid tankard below by Frederick Bassett features a crenulated lip on the lid and a fish-tail terminal on the handle. This style was most prevalent in New York.

The tankard at the bottom right illustrates a style only found in the Philadelphia area. This piece is struck with the *LOVE* touchmark which was used by John Andrew Brunstrom and a succession of eastern Pennsylvania pewterers. The high dome and multiple fillets exhibit a strong Scandinavian influence.

Style

Porringers are shallow bowls with a single handle or, in rare cases, multiple handles. They came in a variety of styles and sizes.

The tab handle porringer to the left was made exclusively in Pennsylvania. It has a basin style bowl and features a handle cast in place.

The crown or "coronet" porringer below has a bulbous bowl with a central "boss" and features a burnt-on handle. This handle style originated in England, but was reproduced in North America during the 18th and early 19th centuries.

The small, crescent or "heart" handle porringer to the bottom left was a popular style in New England during the early 1800s.

Style

The three sugar bowls here demonstrate how styles changed over time.

On the right is a sugar bowl by Thomas Danforth II of Connecticut. This smaller style was popular during the mid to late 18th century in New England.

During the Federal time period, sugar bowls started to become larger and more ornate, as shown in the example below by Parks Boyd of Philadelphia.

The sugar bowl at the bottom was made by George Richardson of Rhode Island. This 19th century piece has handles and a much more contemporary appearance.

Period

The design and construction of a particular piece can often help identify the time period during which it was made. This is illustrated by the teapots on these pages.

The English "skittle ball" teapot to the left was made in the early 18th century while the low dome English teapot below, with its Queen Anne styling, was popular in the mid-1700s.

During the 1750s and 1760s, the dome grew higher and the Queen Anne style became more refined as seen in the English export teapot by Henry Joseph at the bottom.

Period

The drum-shaped teapot to the right by William Will, with its straight spout and beaded decoration, was popular during the American Federal period (1790–1830).

In the early 19th century, teapots became taller. The "transitional style" teapot below by Samuel Kilbourn of Baltimore, Maryland utilized two identical body castings to create this inverted mold form.

By the 1830s and 1840s, most teapots were manufactured from Britannia metal. While the majority of makers continued to cast parts in molds, some turned to stamping or spinning components. The teapot to the right below incorporates early Victorian-era design influences.

Rarity

Rarity is an important factor in collecting antique pewter. It has a strong influence on the desirability and cost of certain items.

Below is a large, three and a half pint tankard by John Bassett of New York. American tankards of this size are extremely rare and this one features a larger handle than other examples, making it the only one known.

Rarity

One of the rarest forms of American 18th century teapots is the oval design shown here. This one is by Francis Bassett I who worked in New York from 1720–1758. There are other marked examples by the Bassetts and one similar example made by William Kirby. A few unmarked teapots in this style also exist.

While 18th century English export teapots are a bit more common, all American teapots from the same time period are considered scarce. They are highly sought after by collectors and difficult to find.

Rarity

While American pint mugs are not rare, the 18th century Boston mug with fish-tail terminal to the left is an exception. Approximately twelve mugs like this one are known to exist.

The 12¼ inch baptismal bowl below is unique. This one-of-a-kind bowl by Henry Will of New York has no other American counterpart. Bowls with a wavy brim and an applied edge were made by pewterers on the European continent, but a matching piece to this handsome dish has yet to be discovered.

Rarity

Pennsylvania pewterer Johann Christoph Heyne advertised porringers as part of his inventory. Yet to date, this is the only one ever found. The "Old English" handle was a common style during the 18th century, but other than William Will and possibly Cornelius Bradford, no other Pennsylvania pewterers were known to have made porringers with this kind of handle.

The fluted "sweetmeat" dish below is one of only two known. This dish, engraved with the date 1728, was made in New York by a member of the Bassett family. It was made by reforming and fluting a cast plate. The elaborate engraving on the front most likely indicates this was a special order made for presentation.

Function

Like plastics today, pewter was once fashioned into many utilitarian objects of the time. To a serious collector, it is important to know what these objects are and how they were used.

The small, 19th century pewter fluid lamp to the left is an example of what is often called a "bed" or "sparking" lamp. Frequently moved from room to room, the small fluid reservoir only allowed a short period of illumination. The finger loop provided an easy way to carry the lamp.

The round, lidded shaving box below is unmarked, but may have been made by Ashbil Griswold of Meriden, Connecticut. Used much like a can of compressed shaving cream is now, the bowl under the lid was separated into two compartments – one for the soap and one for mixing the lather. As a result, this object was both practical and portable.

Function

Using pewter-made eating and drinking objects began at a very early age. To the right is an early 19th century nursing bottle. A forerunner of today's plastic nursing bottles, this item featured a removable cap with nipple.

Below is what is commonly called an infusion pot. In essence, this was an early inhaler, used when people contracted a cold or chest infection.

Herbs and other medicinals were mixed with hot water and added to the pot. An animal skin or flexible rubber tube was attached to the lid and the patient would then inhale the steaming vapors. The pierced, movable cover on the lid was located over a small compartment where camphor was sometimes used.

Condition

Like other antiques, condition plays an important role in collecting pewter. Scale, pitting, abrasions and excessive wear often detract from pewter. And, while some individuals prefer a "worn out" look, many experienced collectors look for pewter in good condition.

Below is a New England strap-handle mug by Nathanial Austin in superb condition. One should never dismiss a mug of this style solely because of condition, but finding an 18th century piece this clean is quite rare. As a result, its corresponding value is very high.

Condition

Today, late 18th century American made porringers are plentiful, but English export porringers from the same period are quite scarce; especially one in this condition.

In America, porringers were in use long after they fell from favor in England. However, some English makers continued producing porringers for export because of their continued popularity abroad.

This "flowered handle" porringer by Hale & Sons of Bristol is practically new and, in fact, may have never been used. Both the handle and bowl are in excellent shape, and the mark is perfectly struck.

Condition

Pewter used for ecclesiastical purposes is often found in good condition.

Communion services usually consisted of a flagon, two chalices or beakers, and at least one paten (plate). Depending on the size of the congregation, additional similar pieces would make up a larger service. Other items might include a basin or baptismal bowl and a ewer (pitcher).

The tall beaker to the right by Samuel Danforth of Hartford, and the Boardman plate below, may very well have originated in a church service. They were obviously handled with great care and consequently, remain in excellent condition.

Condition

Judging Condition at a Glance

The plate below is a composite image which serves to illustrate four
varying degrees of condition: Poor, Good, Better and Best.

Best: A clean and smooth original surface
with few or no defects, makes this plate
highly desirable.

Poor: Scale, pitting (caused by "tin pest"),
scratches, cut marks and numerous abrasions
make this plate much less desirable.

Better: A few minor pits and superficial surface
abrasions make this plate well worth collecting.

Good: Some pitting, less scratches and cut
marks make this plate more acceptable.

Marks

Identifying and understanding touchmarks on pewter is an integral part of becoming a knowledgeable collector.

To the right are the marks of Townsend & Compton, major English exporters in the late 18th and early 19th centuries. In addition to the maker's mark, the Rose and Crown touchmark is often found on English pewter, especially export flatware.[1]

It is important to note, however, that some early American pewterers utilized the Rose and Crown symbols as well. Therefore, one should become familiar with as many marks as possible in order to distinguish between British and American makers.

Below is the touchmark of Bush & Perkins. Located in Bristol, this firm was another important English exporter in the late 18th century. The seated Britannia figure with staff is a symbol found primarily on English pewter.

Reference

1. The Rose and Crown touchmark is also found on some Dutch Pewter.
   see Dubbe, *Tin en Tinnegieters in Nederland*. p. 454

Marks

To the right is the small touchmark of Gershom Jones. Jones was an American maker located in Providence, Rhode Island. The rampant lion is a decidedly English icon, but prior to the American Revolution, several domestic pewterers made use of the figure as well. American use of this symbol illustrates the colonies' close ties with Great Britain at the time.

Animals, scrolls, banners and floral designs were often used by American pewterers during the 18th century. Pictured below is the mark of Samuel Hamlin. Hamlin worked in Connecticut and Rhode Island from 1768 to 1801. This mark was also utilized by his son, Samuel E. Hamlin. Hamlin Jr. worked until 1856 and it is often impossible to determine which Hamlin produced a particular item.

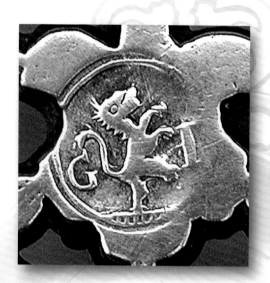

Marks

After the American Revolution, domestic pewterers began using the eagle icon on their work. The newly designated national symbol was a source of great pride for the fledgling nation.

William Will of Philadelphia employed this eagle mark early in the Federal Period. Will used numerous touchmarks during his illustrious career, but this mark is unique. Only one example is known to exist.

Marks

Regional symbols are very rare. Newport, Rhode Island was a major American seaport during the 1700s and the anchor remains the state symbol to this day.

This well-struck mark with an anchor originated with David Melville of Newport (1776–1794). It was most likely used by his brother Thomas, and later by David's son, Thomas.

In addition to identification, touchmarks were an early form of advertising for pewterers. Today, a good touchmark on antique pewter adds significant value to most pieces.

Marks

In addition to the Rose and Crown, early American pewterers occasionally included a *LONDON* mark on their work. This can often be a source of mistaken identity for beginning collectors. The *LOVE* bird mark to the right was used by a number of eastern Pennsylvania makers during the 18th and early 19th centuries. Because England produced the world's most highly regarded pewter at the time, it is thought that some domestic pewterers included the *LONDON* mark to denote comparable quality, both in metal and in finishing.

As American makers switched to the eagle icon during the late 18th and early 19th centuries, the symbol continually evolved. To the bottom right is the well-developed eagle mark by Thomas Danforth III of Connecticut and Philadelphia. This and other eagle marks closely follow American coin designs of the time.

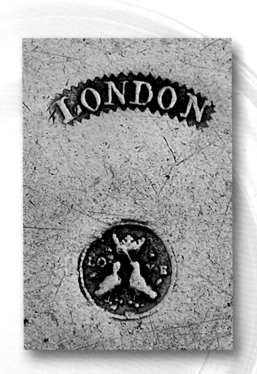

Marks

In the 1820s and 30s, pewter manfacturing became more industrialized. This was caused, in part, by the increasing competition of chinaware and other ceramics for eating and drinking. With increased production, touchmarks were simplified. Straight line marks using last names or initials (stamped or incised) were commonplace throughout this period.

To the right is the mark of Boardman & Hart. While the Boardmans continued to manufacture most of their pewter in Hartford, Connecticut, they expanded their sales and marketing to both New York and Philadelphia. Whether this mark was applied before or after delivery to New York is uncertain.

Allen Porter, along with his brother Freeman, produced a number of Britannia ware styles in Maine during the mid-1800s. The serrated rectangle mark below is an excellent example of similar marks struck by pewterers at the time.

Marks

'Hallmarks' on pewter first appeared during the middle of the 17th century. The use of 'hallmarks' copied a long standing tradition established by goldsmiths and silversmiths, but had little relevance on pewter. However, in many instances at least one of the 'hallmarks' was distinctive enough to help identify a specific maker.

To the left are the 'hallmarks' of English pewterer Thomas Giffin, later used by the London partnership of Townsend & Giffin. 'Hallmarks' are generally found on flatware, but are sometimes found on 17th and 18th century hollowware, such as tankards and mugs.

Below are the 'hallmarks' of Thomas Danforth II who worked in Middletown, Connecticut from 1755 to 1782. His son, Thomas Danforth III, also used these 'hallmarks' following his father's death. The symbols closely follow standard British icons of the same time period. The use of 'hallmarks' on American pewter began to fade in the early 19th century.

Marks

There are other ancillary marks sometimes found on pewter that collectors should become familiar with.

Owner's initials, as illustrated on the plate to the right, were occasionally struck on sets of flatware. Generally located on the front rim, two or three letter designations were the norm. Owner's initials should not be confused with maker's marks.

To the right is an *X* mark with a Timothy Boardman & Company touchmark below. Also pictured above the Thomas Giffin 'hallmarks' on the facing page, use of the *X* or crowned *X* on both English and American pewter denotes quality. An *X* commonly signified the use of a higher proportion of tin in the pewter.

The crowned *VR* below and crowned *WR* on the opposite page are known as verification marks. These marks were struck to confirm and standardize capacity, which was strictly regulated in England. Verification marks of any kind on American pewter are extremely rare.

Decoration

Decoration can add much interest and significant value to pewter.

Below is a 24 inch, early 18th century dish by English pewterer Thomas Powell. The dish features an engraved scene depicting St. George slaying a dragon. This is a good example of straight line engraving. Much the same as engraving done on silver, this highly sophisticated technique required exceptional talent and considerable skill.

Decoration

To the right are engraved initials on an English export mug. This style of engraved initials is often called "Boston Initials" because pewter with this kind of engraving has been frequently found on pieces with a history in the Boston area. There are varied degrees of quality known in these engraved initials, which indicates more than one person did this work.

Below is an example of standard straight line engraving and what is commonly known as "bright cut" engraving, found on a 19th century Boardman teapot.

In the detail inset, bright cut engraving is seen on the foliate frame surrounding the cross-hatched oval and on the leaves of the flowering plant. To accomplish this technique, the engraver used a tool – known as a graver – with a curved or scooped point. By varying the degree of pressure, the engraver could control the depth, width and sharpness of the cut.[2]

Reference

2. Pass, JG. "Folk Art Engraving on Pewter". *The Bulletin*, PCCA, Vol. 13, No. 1, p. 5.

Decoration

While less common, folk art engraving is another style of decoration used on pewter. Folk art engraving is generally found on utilitarian items likes mugs and plates. The techniques vary, but the designs tend to be more simplistic and somewhat primitive.

To the right is a crude, but rather charming eagle engraved on the front of a Boardman mug.[3] Folk art engraving on American pewter is quite rare.

The folk art scene on the German plate below depicts Adam and Eve in the Garden of Good and Evil. Biblical motifs are often found on decorated flatware from continental Europe.

Reference

3. Pass, JG. "Folk Art Engraving on Pewter". *The Bulletin*, PCCA, Vol. 13, No. 1, p. 17.

Decoration

Wrigglework is a more common form of engraving on period pewter. Both the tool and technique required are different from those used for straight line engraving. A short, flat ended rod with a wooden handle, much like a screwdriver, is used to produce a zigzag pattern in the metal.[4]

To the right is a rare, 17th century Dutch beaker depicting the coronation of William & Mary. The workmanship of the wrigglework decoration is simple, yet well designed and executed.

The Seder dish below is of German origin. The wrigglework engraving includes several ingredients of the Passover meal surrounding a Pascal lamb. Inscriptions in Hebrew are engraved around the rim.

Reference

4. Pass, JG. "Folk Art Engraving on Pewter". *The Bulletin*, PCCA, Vol. 13, No. 1, p. 6.

Decoration

Cast decoration is a far more elaborate form of decoration on pewter. In this case, the design is actually cut into the mold prior to casting, thus producing a three dimensional relief when finished.

With the exception of spoons, cast decoration on American pewter is exceedingly rare. To the left is the detail of a spoon handle by Luther Boardman of East Haddam, Connecticut. Luther Boardman produced thousands of spoons in the 19th century, many with early Victorian design elements.

Below is a very rare 18th century, two-handled Communion cup attributed to Robert Bonynge of Boston. While the gadrooned ribbing at the bottom is sometimes found on English hollowware, only this American maker may have produced cups with this style of cast decoration.

Decoration

Beading is a style of decoration that became popular during the American Federal period. By using a knurling tool, the maker could apply a series of beads along the outside edge of finials, lids, bases, and connection points along the body.

To the right is a late 18th century coffeepot, unmarked, but certainly of Philadelphia manufacture. Overall, this piece includes thirteen rows of beaded decoration, some of which can be seen more clearly in the detail photo below. Beaded decoration is also found on tankards, teapots, chalices, creamers, sugar bowls and salts from the same period.

Attribution

A considerable amount of American pewter is unmarked. Yet much of it can be attributed to a specific maker by comparing certain elements of an unmarked piece to that of a marked piece. The pewter displayed on these two pages helps to demonstrate that ability.

To the far left is a marked 19th century flagon by Israel Trask. Next to it is an unmarked chalice. Pewterers often used one mold to cast different parts for different pieces. The inset photos at the bottom show how Trask used the lid of his flagon to create the base of the chalice. The height, diameter and shape are an exact match. Since molds were expensive, the use of interchangable parts enabled makers to create a variety of forms and styles. And, it provides those who study pewter today with an effective way to attribute unmarked ware.

Attribution

The porringers on this page are by William Will of Philadelphia. One is marked and one is unmarked. While the "Old English" (sometimes called "New York") handle style was not uncommon in America during the 18th century, Will's version of it is quite distinctive. The round apertures at the bottom of the handle are found on porringers by both William and his father John. However, the wide neck "doughnut" shaped hanging portion of the handle is a feature exclusive to William.[5] By comparing the handle of the marked porringer to that of the unmarked porringer, one is able to, without reservation, attribute the unmarked piece to William Will.

Reference
5. Wolf, Melvyn D., M.D. "New York Handle Porringers, A Method of Identification".
   The Bulletin, PCCA, Vol. 12, No. 6, pp. 262–263.

Construction & Fabrication

Construction & Fabrication

A general knowledge of the construction methods used in the manufacture of antique pewter is of importance to both the novice and the seasoned collector. Having a good understanding of the manufacturing process aids in determining whether or not a piece is legitimate.

What is pewter? Pewter is an alloy of the element tin to which a number of other elements are added in varying amounts to achieve different qualities of the alloy which makes this metal suitable for many uses. The elements that were most frequently added are copper, antimony, lead and bismuth. Occasionally pieces are found that are made of nearly pure tin. These pieces have a tendency to develop stress cracks or fractures as tin alone is quite brittle. Adding the aforementioned elements strengthens the alloy and makes it more resilient and easier to machine or hand finish. For example, copper added in small amounts results in a harder metal which is less susceptible to cracking. Lead softens the metal and makes it more pliable and easier to finish. Alloys with more copper and antimony have a tendency to be strong and lustrous, whereas those with a greater quantity of lead are softer in appearance and strength.

Antique pewter was produced by four basic methods of production. These methods are casting, spinning, stamping, and hand fabrication from sheet metal. Casting is achieved by pouring molten metal into a mold. Molds were primarily made of bronze. However, other materials including steel, soapstone, plaster, and wood were also used. Spinning is the forcing of sheet metal over a form in a lathe to produce a desired part or whole object. Stamping required striking a sheet of pewter between a male and female die resulting in the desired form. Lastly, some pewter was formed from sheet metal in much the same manner as a silver object. The pewterer would use a template to cut out a specific part from sheet metal that would then be shaped by hand over a wood form and soldered at the joint. Other parts would be formed by hand or by the spinning process to complete the parts for the item being made.

Cast metal has a property that distinguishes it from stamped or spun metal. If a piece of cast pewter is held by an edge and tapped with one's fingernail, there is a distinct "ring" to the metal. Tapping stamped and spun metal, on the other hand, produces a dull "thud". This is important to remember when examining certain pieces of pewter. For example, all period porringers have cast bowls whereas many fakes and most reproductions have spun bowls. If one taps a porringer bowl and hears a dull thud, be advised that the piece is likely not period.

Spinning and stamping are developments of the late 18th century, which were perfected in the 19th century. These new manufacturing techniques allowed for a wider variety of designs to be introduced and ushered in true "assembly line" production. But, regardless of whatever method was employed, the primary advantage to the manufacturer was that absolutely identical pieces could be produced. Identical parts also allowed the pewterer to often use a single type of casting for multiple purposes. For instance, a casting from a tankard lid mold might be used for the foot of a chalice or the lid of a sugar bowl. This technique was later employed in the machine tool industry.

Recognizing and understanding the types of construction used by particular makers can aid in determining if a piece is authentic. For example, Parks Boyd, a Philadelphia maker, made only cast pewter. A spun piece of pewter with Parks Boyd marks should cause a collector to suspect its authenticity!

Although most pewterers marked much of their production, a considerable amount of pewter was made unmarked. Knowledge of construction methods, molds and forms used by various pewterers aids in attribution to a particular maker or family of pewterers.

The following pages further illustrate construction and fabrication methods, and provide more information about all aspects of the manufacturing process.

Casting

The fact that pewter is easily cast in molds makes it an ideal metal for producing a wide variety of forms. The metal also picks up details of designs such as surface decorations on spoons. Fine details, as found in thumbpiece and handle designs, make this metal the perfect candidate.

Pewter melts at a temperature range of around 450 to 600 degrees Fahrenheit, depending on the particular alloy.

The ideal casting temperature also depends on the particular alloy. A metal that melts around 450 to 500 degrees might cast best at a temperature of around 550 degrees.

Pewter alloys vary widely in their make-up. The prime element in pewter is tin. Other elements including copper, antimony and bismuth, as well as lead, were added in various quantities to produce alloys best designed for specific purposes. Fine quality alloys used in the best hollowware would contain tin along with small amounts of copper, a little antimony and small amounts of lead or no lead at all. An alloy for measures that only held liquids for short periods of time might contain considerably more lead. It is important to note that once a metal has been alloyed, it is difficult to separate into its component ingredients. Therefore, it is unlikely that copper or lead would leach out of the alloy. Pewterers developed the alloys that worked best in the molds they had and for the uses they intended.

Casting

Pictured on the preceding page is a bronze mold for casting basins. The bottom left image shows the mold in the closed position, while above it the mold is open. Note the sprue gate on the side of the mold. This is where the molten metal was poured into the mold. The inset photo illustrates a finished basin by Samuel Hamlin set in the mold.

To the right, we see examples of pewter during the finishing process. In the foreground of the inset photo there is a basin with the sprue still attached. The sprue is excess metal left in the pouring gate.

Below we see a spoon mold with a freshly cast spoon still in the mold. Note the sprue at the end of the bowl of the spoon and the "flashing" around the edges of the spoon handle. Flashing is where molten metal leaked outside of the mold cavity.

Multiple Mold Casting

Plates, dishes, and basins along with Pennsylvania tab handle porringers were each produced from a single casting made in a two-part mold. Nearly every other form made of pewter, was made from multiple finished castings assembled together to make a single object. These are known as complex forms. Complex forms include mugs, beakers, flagons, teapots, creamers, sugar bowls, etc..

The photographs below show some of the molds necessary to produce one of these complex forms, a tankard.

This form required six separate molds. There are molds for the body, base, lid, thumbpiece, handle, and hinge pin. The pewterer would cast as many separate castings of each part as needed for his production quota. Each part was finished and assembled to create the complete tankard shown on the opposite page.

Slush Casting

Slush casting is the method by which a pewterer produces a hollow form without a center core to the mold. This is the general method by which handles and hollow spouts are made. Many candlestick and chalice shafts are also produced in this manner.

These molds generally consist of two halves with a long pouring gate at one or both ends. Initially, molten metal is poured into the closed mold. The pewterer waited a few seconds until the metal began to congeal, then dumped the remaining molten metal out of the mold into the melting pot (see the inset photo below). The result is a hollow casting.

This method allowed for complex curved forms like handles to be made in a single casting rather than in halves, which had to be soldered together. Hollow handles also reduced the amount of metal needed for the job, making the part lighter in weight and easier to solder to the body of the object being produced.

Trimming, Skimming and Finishing

A pewter casting taken directly from the mold requires finishing. Some parts were lathe finished while others were finished by hand. Various tools were required to complete this process. A grouping of some of these pewterer's tools is shown below. Circular or cylindrical pewter castings including basins, for example, were lathe finished. The casting was affixed to a form on the lathe and then the pewterer would "skim" the casting with a tool hand held against a tool rest. The cutting tools used were designed for this purpose.

The skimming process is very similar to the way a joiner lathe turns a chair leg. In some cases, the skimmed piece would also be "burnished" using a highly polished steel tool with a blunt end specifically designed for this purpose. Burnishing produces very fine and even "turning" marks, while skimming leaves broader and coarser marks. The inset photo on the opposite page illustrates turning marks on a plate.

Handles, spouts, thumbpieces and spoons, etc. were finished by hand scraping and hand burnishing as well.

The photo below shows a sprue being removed from a spoon casting. The sprue and flashing (excess pewter) were generally cut off by hand using shears.

Complex forms, including mugs and teapots, required the finishing of a number of pieces both by the turning and hand finish methods.

Trimming, Skimming and Finishing

Directly below is a basin being skimmed on a lathe. Note the tool on the rest and the shavings coming off the casting. This process cleans off slight imperfections in the casting leaving a bright finish. Later the surface might be burnished to produce an even finer finish.

From the 17th through the early 19th centuries, the skimming process took place on a lathe with a large, hand-cranked wheel or on a foot-powered treadle lathe.

The inset photo to the right below clearly illustrates the concentric circles of turning marks on the surface of a plate.

To the left and below, an inset photo shows a pewterer sanding off the end of the spoon where the sprue was removed. Throughout the 18th century and early 19th century, this was done by hand with a file and scrapers. By the mid-19th century, belt driven machinery allowed for more modern and time saving finishing techniques.

Assembly

Complex form pieces are comprised of many parts. The pewterer had to determine the best sequence of finishing each part and the subsequent order in which they were best assembled.

The two body parts of the teapot (shown below) would have been finished on the inside prior to their being joined together. In the inset photo to the right, Master Pewterer Richard Graver joins the body parts using a hot soldering iron with a linen pad held against the inside to keep the metal in place. The resulting seam has the linen impression on the inside of the pot.

The outer surface was then finished, "dressing off" the irregular surface that the soldering iron would leave.

The spout was "sweat soldered" on. This required holding the finished spout against the body (over the strainer holes); small pieces of low temperature melt solder were placed at the joint and fluxed. A torch was used to heat and melt the solder which would "run" around the joint.

The wood handle was affixed to ferrules (pewter collars), fitted to the body and sweat soldered on. The two parts of the hinge were drilled, pinned and sweat soldered to the lid and upper body. The result: a completed teapot.

Assembly

The photo, below-right, shows a handle being "burned on" to a porringer body. The pewterer would completely finish the bowl for the porringer. Porringer tongs, padded with linen, would be clamped to the inside of the finished bowl. When the handles of these tongs were closed, the jaws opened outward thus ensuring a tight fit of the linen against the inside of the bowl.

The pewterer and his journeymen would apply the handle. One man would steady the bowl by holding the tongs. Another man would hold the two-part handle mold (seen below) in place on the upper edge of the bowl while a third man poured molten metal into the mold.

The molten metal would run into the mold and come into contact with the upper outside edge of the porringer bowl. The heat from the molten metal would melt through the bowl at this junction. The linen on the inner edge of the bowl held this molten metal in place. The mold was filled to the top. The upper left photo shows the resulting "linen mark".

Next, the handle mold was removed from the casting, and the flashing and sprue were then trimmed. Sometimes, the handles were finished by "planishing" also known as hammering. Planishing was a technique that had generally ceased being used by the end of the 18th century.

Hammering

The process of hammering or planishing pewter exemplifies one of the highest and most prized skills in the art of the pewterer. A planishing hammer was struck against the surface of the booge while it was held closely against a "hammering stake". This allowed the worker to make clear hammer marks without distorting the shape of the object.

In England, there existed the Company of Hammermen. These highly skilled workers were employed to hammer the booges of plates, dishes, and basins. In some cases, the entire surface of a piece would be hammered (see photo of dish to the left below). Occasionally, this also included hollowware. There are examples of tankards that have had the drum hammered all over.

The process of hammering not only creates an attractive surface, it also strengthens the metal by making the density more consistent and less susceptible to cracks.

Hammering of the booge is almost always seen on pieces of English manufacture from the very early periods through the first portion of the 19th century. In America, however, it is seen only until the end of the 18th century, and only by a limited number of makers. Hammering is also found on pieces of European manufacture.

Striking Marks

Below are pictured two examples of pewterers' dies. One is the small eagle touchmark of Samuel Pierce of Greenfield, Mass., circa 1792–1830, and the other is a "crowned *X*" touchmark. Dies were hand-cut from some of the best steel available in order to endure the repeated hits from the hammer used to impress the die into the pewter object.

After the desired piece was finished, either skimmed, or skimmed and burnished, the maker struck his mark. On porringer handles, however, finishing was not necessary and not always done prior to striking the mark. A touchmark was often struck on the base of a piece of hollowware before assembly. This was done because it might be difficult to strike the touchmark after the object was assembled.

When the pewterer struck his mark, he placed the object to be marked against a polished steel anvil, held his die firmly against the pewter object, and struck the die with a hammer. Sometimes the die did not hit squarely on the surface and only a partial touchmark resulted.

Pewterers often had name touchmarks like the Pierce die, and other dies that might indicate the city where they worked. For example, there are city dies for London, Boston, New York, Middletown (Connecticut), as well as others. *X* marks are found with and without crowns.

Other Manufacturing Techniques

The 19th century ushered in the Industrial Revolution and pewter manufacturing took advantage of new production methods. The fact that pewter cast in a mold resulted in absolutely identical objects every time shows that pewterers were already ahead in their manufacturing techniques. Most 19th century manufacturing included some precision machine work on each of the component parts. However, since some components were still cast, assembly was generally less exacting.

New methods for forming component parts expanded the ways in which pewter was made. To the left below, we see a steel engraving of a worker "drop forging" a component part. A male die was dropped onto a piece of pewter over a female die. The impact forced the metal to conform to the female die resulting in an identical product every time this was done.

The component parts were trimmed of any excess metal and assembled to form a whole object. It is likely the panels that make up the body of the teapot below were formed by this drop forge method.

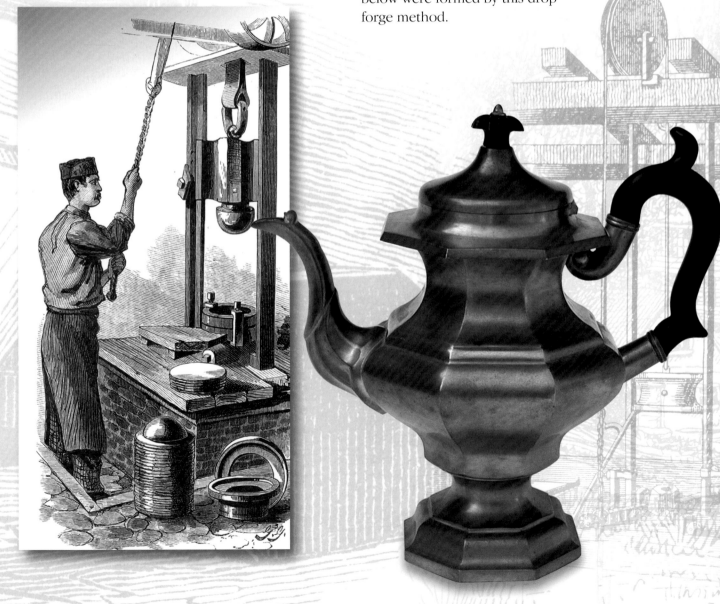

Other Manufacturing Techniques

Pewter has the wonderful property of being able to be rolled into sheet metal. The sheet metal can be cut into discs and "spun" over wood or metal forms to produce identical items each time.

The form or "chuck" is attached to a lathe. A sheet of pewter is centered at the end of the chuck and held in place by the tail-stock. Using a highly polished steel spinning tool (as seen to the right), the pewterer then forced the metal to conform to the form of the chuck. This process required a considerable amount of pressure. The tool is braced against a post on the lathe rest and slowly forced against the spinning pewter.

After the initial spinning is accomplished, the pewterer will finish off the edges, either completing the form, or making it ready for inclusion as a part to be assembled with other parts.

A multi-part chuck for making porringer bowls, along with a finished porringer, is pictured in the small inset photo below.

To the left, Jon Gibson, a contemporary pewterer from New Hampshire, is shown spinning pewter at his lathe. Spinning pewter is performed essentially the same way it was done in the 19th century, as illustrated below in the circa 1878 steel engraving.

Fakes, Forgeries & Reproductions

Fakes, Forgeries & Reproductions

As a nationally recognized dealer in antique pewter, John Carl Thomas was keenly aware of the prevalence of spurious pieces in the marketplace. In the late 1970s, John began to assemble a "Study Collection" for the Pewter Collectors' Club of America. On occasion, John would present some of these "fakes" to study groups at pewter club meetings. His expert knowledge of the subject allowed him to present the reasons why a particular piece was "bad" in a clear and concise manner. As the collection grew, it became apparent that this assembly of objects was too important and valuable a tool to restrict to club members only. Thus the PCCA decided to spread this knowledge and publish much of the available information. It is also important to note that much of the descriptive text for the pieces illustrated in this portion of the book was rewritten from recorded comments dictated by John Carl Thomas. Additional descriptive text was written by current PCCA Authenticity Chairman, Wayne A. Hilt.

The term "fakes" encompasses a wide variety of examples and there are many methods by which fakers produce them. Striking a spurious or "pseudo" mark of a period pewterer on an unmarked period piece is one method of producing a fake. Some of the fake dies for striking these pseudo maker's marks are very well executed, while others are poor reproductions. Over time, a serious collector will learn what period touchmarks look like. However, a photo comparison to a legitimate mark is the best method to prevent being fooled. This is true for the experienced collector well as the novice collector.

Taking parts from several period pieces and constructing a new form is another type of fake. This combination of parts is referred to as a "marriage". Sometimes fakers will strike a spurious touchmark on a reproduction piece of pewter to fool collectors. Cutting out a legitimate touchmark from a damaged piece of pewter and insetting it into a more valuable form is another tool of the deceiver. This chapter illustrates and discusses many examples of these various types of fakes.

A forgery or counterfeit is a piece of modern pewter specifically made with the intent of deceiving the collector. These are created using several different methods. One method is to produce an object and strike a faked die mark of a period pewterer onto the piece. Another technique of the forger is to use a mold produced from a legitimate period piece and cast one or more exact copies. The resulting mold, sometimes made of plaster or silicon rubber, has every knife mark and other imperfection that exists on the original piece, including touchmarks. These can be difficult to spot as forgeries, even for an experienced collector. Fortunately, if more than one example was made, each one is an exact clone of all the others, with the same scratches, pits and touchmarks.

A reproduction is a modern copy of a piece of antique pewter, following *general period designs*, using both early and contemporary, materials and techniques. On occasion, today's pewterers will produce *exact* copies of specific items. In both cases, these modern reproductions are marked by the maker so as not to deceive the public.

Occasionally, faked pewter was cast in molds of poor quality resulting in a "muddy" appearance to the details. These pieces are in contrast to the highly defined details generally found on period castings made in bronze molds. Also, much faked pewter was not lathe finished like period pewter resulting in a lack of crispness.

Some faked pewter has been put inside a tumbler, along with foreign materials, in order to leave little nicks and dents in the surface. This method has a tendency to leave distress over the entire surface of the object, including areas that would usually show no wear on a legitimate period piece. For example, the bottom surface protected by the foot of a footed bowl would most likely show little or no wear.

One must also be aware of color in examining a piece of pewter. Some fakes have been deliberately oxidized to give the piece an "antique" appearance. Differences of opinion among collectors regarding "color" are reflected in the argument of whether or not to clean antique pewter. Many collectors believe that antique pewter should be cleaned, because that was the way pewter was generally kept during the period of its daily use. Another school of thought is to leave the color and patina that have been acquired with age. This results in an "old look". Much fake pewter has had "artificial color" chemically placed on the surface, resulting in a false old look. Consequently, one must be cautious when selecting pewter with a dark, uncleaned appearance.

A few years ago, The (British) Pewter Society, in its efforts to educate the collecting audience, published a book entitled *The Richard Neate Touch Plate and two others of unknown origin*. Richard Neate was a dealer in both legitimate and faked pewter during the early 20th century. The book includes photographs of the touchplate struck with the fake marks allegedly produced and used by Richard Neate. Also included are photos of two unknown fake touchplates. A section of the book shows photographs of the period mark alongside the fake mark for comparison. This volume incorporates the same technique.

In summation, it is extremely important to be aware of the wide scope of information available to collectors on fakes and forgeries. All collectors, from the beginner to the seasoned veteran, need to keep all of this data in mind when making decisions about adding an item to their collection. This chapter will help to expand that growing body of knowledge.

Mugs & Chalices

19th Century Mug with a Fake James Putnam Mark

19th Century Mug with a Fake James Putnam Mark

This is a pint capacity ale or beer mug, 4^5/$_{16}$ inches high and roughly 3^1/$_4$ inches at the upper diameter, with a reeded/stepped base. One often finds these in Eastern New England. They were probably made by a pewterer around the Boston area, or perhaps even as far north as Portland, Maine.

The handle looks much later than the rest of the beaker style body. It is a single long curve with Victorian decoration used as a thumb rest on the back of the handle. But, these beakers are found in some quantity and the only one that has ever been seen marked correctly was by a firm that has never been identified – Whitehouse and Woodbury.

This particular example bears a fake mark of James Putnam on the bottom within a serrated rectangle. The fake mark is a little larger than a genuine Putnam mark. Put side by side with a real Putnam mark, the fake mark is readily identifiable.

Fake James Putnam mark

Genuine James Putnam mark

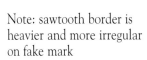

Note: sawtooth border is heavier and more irregular on fake mark

Note: angle on left side of the "A" in the fake mark is more pronounced than in the genuine mark

Serifs on letters in the correct mark are smaller and more refined

Fake 18th Century Mug by Richard Neate

This Griffin's head is a known
Richard Neate hallmark

Fake 18th Century Mug by Richard Neate

This is a mug of approximately one pint capacity, vaguely in the shape of an hourglass, with a very wide middle section. The overall height of the mug is 5³/₈ inches. The bottom diameter is 3¹³/₁₆ inches as is the top diameter. One could liken the shape to the general outline of a Tappit Hen (Scottish measure), although in this particular case, it is even at the top and bottom. This mug is an inverted mold form; the two parts are joined at the very middle of the mug at the narrowest point of the body. The top and the bottom are exactly the same with the exception of a solid part being inserted into the bottom.

The piece has various marks. There is a *LONDON* mark, an *X* and crown, and some other 20th century hallmarks around the rim. One mark is the face of a leopard staring straight ahead. Another is a Griffin's head, a mark known to have been used by Richard Neate (a similar mark also appears on the porringer on page 116). All three devices are to the left of the handle. The handle in this case is a double-C scroll handle with a very finely done acanthus leaf across the top. It is very similar to handle types used in early British pewter.

There is no question that this piece was made by Richard Neate or his associates. It has been artificially colored and artificially distressed.

20th Century Chalices with a Fake Mark

20th Century Chalices with a Fake Mark

These are a pair of 9¹¹/₁₆ inch tall chalices with a base diameter of 4⁷/₈ inches. They have a double-domed base and a large suppressed ball knop stem. The bottom and the top of the stem are essentially the same casting, joined in the middle of the suppressed ball. A large bell-shaped cup is attached to the upper portion of the stem. Each of these chalices bears on the side, a waisted oval die with a rose and crown and the words *MADE IN* above and *LONDON* below.

These chalices were made in the early 20th century in at least two different sizes. The oxide is artificial and they were a form probably meant to deceive.

Note: scratches and pitting are too uniform indicating artificial aging

This touchmark is made to appear "of period" and coupled with artificial oxide, defines this piece as a fake

19th Century Chalice with a Fake Israel Trask Mark

19th Century Chalice with a Fake Israel Trask Mark

This chalice or church cup has an over-all height of 5³/₈ inches, a top diameter of 3¹/₄ inches, and a bottom diameter of 3¹/₈ inches. This is an American chalice, made close to the middle third of the nineteenth century, probably around Taunton, Massachusetts. But this particular example has a fake mark of Israel Trask on the outside bottom, placed on a convex surface. It is a very poor mark, and is a known fake Trask touchmark.

Trask never made this shape of chalice. Trask's chalices were either beaker form, or an earlier style with an elongated center shaft. He also made thistle-shaped chalices, which are the most common.

Fake Israel Trask mark

Genuine Israel Trask mark

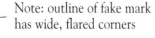

Note: outline of fake mark has wide, flared corners

Note: "R" is dropped and has a different baseline

Serifs on letters in genuine mark are more pronounced

19th Century Chalices with a Fake William Will Mark

19th Century Chalices with a Fake William Will Mark

This is a pair of chalices, 5³/₁₆ inches tall with a top and bottom diameter of 3 inches. These fakes were made by taking a perfectly good pair of mid-19th century, beaker style chalices and striking a fake William Will mark along the lip of the rim. The design is pure 19th century. They were constructed by taking a 3 inch beaker, applying a convex bottom, then attaching a base with a small spool shaft in the middle. All the parts are of cast metal. They are an attractive form, but unlike anything William Will would have produced in the 18th century.

While the placement of the touchmark on the lip is found on some William Will tankards, the overall style of the chalices should be a sign that the fake marks were added later.

When comparing an original Will mark with these fake marks, it becomes readily apparent that the quality of the engraving on the fake marks is inferior.

Fake William Will mark

Genuine William Will mark

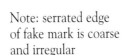

Note: serrated edge of fake mark is coarse and irregular

Small "m" is too large and blocky

Serrated edge of genuine mark is fine and evenly spaced

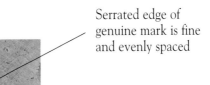

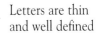

Letters are thin and well defined

19th Century Mug with a Fake George Lightner Mark

Fake George Lightner mark

Genuine George Lightner mark

Note: the fake touchmark has numerous impressions, none of which are clear. This doubling effect was caused by the object not being properly secured when the die was struck.

Note: the clarity of the letters and the border. The feathers on the eagle are crisp

19th Century Mug with a Fake George Lightner Mark

This is a pint capacity mug, 4⁵/₁₆ inches high and roughly 3¹/₄ inches at the upper diameter, with a flared base. The Pewter Collectors' Club of America was most fortunate to acquire this fake for the Study Collection. It is not so important because of the relatively good skill of the individual who produced the fake Lightner die, nor is it very important as a well done fake. In fact, the mug is quite poor overall. What is important is that this is the exact mug pictured in Laughlin's *Pewter in America, Its Makers and Their Marks*, Volume II, Plate LXXVIII, Figure 682 in the section on fakes. Laughlin was one of the first scholars on antique pewter to publish something about fakes. This embryonic effort helped clear the way for more open discussions on the topic of fakes and how to avoid them.

The border of the fake mark is quite well done and the eagle is also fairly well executed. Were the fake mark struck clearly on an appropriate size plate, for example, it would probably fool many collectors. Fortunately, the faker struck the touchmark on a piece that was not of the period.

Beakers

Correct Trask Cup with a Fake TD&SB Mark

Correct Trask Cup with a Fake TD&SB Mark

This shaped beaker or church cup is 3½ inches tall and is typical of the Beverly, Massachusetts area. The cup dates from about 1820. It has bands of engine-turned type decoration common to the shops of both Israel and Oliver Trask, and could safely be attributed to them.

On the outside bottom is a fake mark of Thomas Danforth Boardman and Sherman Boardman – the *TD&SB* mark. This is one of several currently known fake *TD&SB* marks (see pages 74, 78, 111, 112, and 192), and has been applied to many different beakers, porringers and other objects. This particular fake is quite good and closely mimics one of the genuine *TD&SB* marks. This mark, were it struck on a piece of Boardman pewter, could certainly fool a collector.

Incorrect TD&SB mark

Genuine TD&SB mark

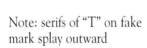

Note: serifs of "T" on fake mark splay outward

The "T" and "D" on the genuine mark are not on the same baseline

Note: the ampersand in the genuine mark is wider

Correct Hamlin Beaker with a Fake Eagle Mark

Correct Hamlin Beaker with a Fake Eagle Mark

This beaker is 3³/₁₆ inches in height. It is marked with a tiny Hamlin mark in a rectangle and is an honest Hamlin quarter-pint beaker. It has a serious melt on the base, but that is not the issue.

The inside bottom of the beaker has a very crude eagle plaque. At one time the eagle mark was considered a rare and unrecorded American touchmark. Even now, no one really knows where that eagle mark came from. It has never been discovered on any other object.

The small Hamlin mark is on the side, up near the rim. The mark is legitimate. Consequently, it is a true Hamlin beaker, but the eagle mark is a fake.

This small genuine Hamlin mark is often missed by novice collectors and dealers alike due to its size and placement. When inspecting a beaker of the exact style and size, be sure to look all around the rim for this mark.

Note: raised bumps are the result of the metal being compressed into defects on the anvil when the fake touchmark was struck on the inside

This attractive eagle touchmark is made to look like an eagle die from the early 19th century. If this appeared on the inside of an unmarked basin or the back of a plate, it might be mistaken for an unrecorded period touchmark.

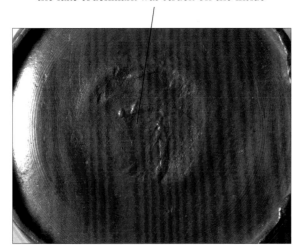

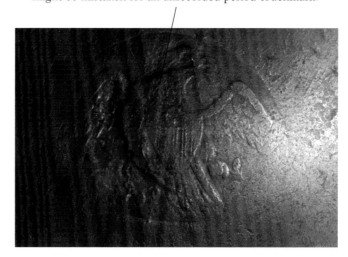

19th Century Beaker with a Fake Richard Lee Mark

This is a standard flared-type beaker, 2½ inches tall and about 2¹³/₁₆ inches at the upper diameter. It is a type of beaker one associates with the time period, from 1830 at the earliest, to 1860 at the latest.

The beaker bears on the inside bottom a fake mark of Richard Lee. A photo of this mark is found in Ledlie Laughlin's *Pewter In America*, Vol. 1, Plate LVI, Figure 413. Laughlin attributed this mark to Lee, but it is incorrect. If one compares this mark with the known, correct, single-line *RICHARD • LEE* mark, one can observe that the genuine mark is a different size and configuration. This fake mark appears on other pieces in this book and will be referred to as L413.

In addition, both Richard Lee, Sr. and Richard Lee, Jr. had been dead for probably 20 years before this beaker could have been made, so that is more proof this piece has a fake mark.

19th Century Beaker with a Fake Richard Lee Mark

Fake Richard Lee mark

Genuine Richard Lee mark

Fake mark has more distance between letters and edge

Note: fake mark has fine, evenly spaced serrations on the sawtooth edge

Letters on genuine mark are irregular and appear hand-cut

Mid-19th Century Beaker with a Fake TD&SB Mark

Mid-19th Century Beaker with a Fake TD&SB Mark

This is another flared beaker or tumbler from the second quarter of the 19th century. This one is 2⅞ inches high and about 2⅞ inches at the top diameter. The beaker is marked on the inside bottom with one of several known fake Thomas Danforth Boardman and Sherman Boardman touchmarks (see pages 71, 78, 111, 112, and 192). It is a style of beaker totally unlike the actual beakers produced by the Boardmans. While the Boardmans did make 3 inch beakers, the shape was different. Likely to be as late as 1860, this beaker was probably produced by a firm like the Meriden Britannia Manufacturing Company. If the Boardmans had made a beaker like this, they most assuredly would not have struck their mark on the inside bottom. This is a very poor fake of the mark. You can see the rectangle has almost turned itself into a bow tie. This mark has been noted on other pieces.

Incorrect TD&SB mark

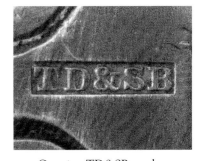

Genuine TD&SB mark

There are at least two known TD&SB marks – One has wide letters (shown here) and one has thin letters (see page 71)

Note: the fake mark has a "horizontal hourglass" shape to the border

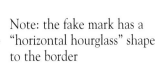

The top and bottom edges of genuine mark are nearly parallel

19th Century Beaker with a Fake Smith & Company Mark

This is a well made flared beaker, a tumbler of the second quarter of the 19th century, (maybe as early as 1825 to 1830). It is precisely 3 inches high with a 2⅞ inch diameter at the top. Unfortunately, it bears a fake mark of *SMITH & CO* in the arched, rectangle design found on the inside bottom of the beaker. Smith & Company, working in the mid to late 1840s, would never have struck their mark in this location on a beaker.

19th Century Beaker with a Fake Smith & Company Mark

Fake Smith & Company mark

Genuine Smith & Company mark

Both ends of the fake touchmark are well rounded and note how close the letters are to the edge of the touchmark

The distance of the letters to the border is greater in the genuine mark

Note: only the right end of the real touch is rounded – the left end is curved on the top edge and angular at the bottom

19th Century Beaker with a Fake Israel Trask Mark

Here is another flared beaker, lightweight, and dating a little later than the middle of the 19th century. It has very thin metal and is pretty well eaten up by oxide. It bears a fake mark of Israel Trask on the inside bottom where, if in fact Trask had made these 3 inch beakers, he would never have placed his mark. This is a relatively well known Trask fake.

19th Century Beaker with a Fake Israel Trask Mark

Fake Israel Trask mark

Genuine Israel Trask mark

Note: outline of fake mark is too far from letters

Note: different shape on right foot of "R"

Serifs on letters in genuine mark are more pronounced

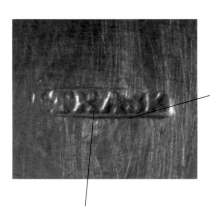

19th Century Handled Beaker with a Fake Israel Trask Mark

19th Century Handled Beaker with a Fake Israel Trask Mark

This is a beaker with a curved handle. The body of the beaker is 2³/₈ inches tall and the upper diameter is about 3 inches. The beaker has a nice S-curved handle, typical of the second quarter of the 19th century, very well made, and bearing the same fake *I•TRASK* touchmark found on another beaker. This mark is on the outside bottom of the beaker where a legitimate Trask mark would be.

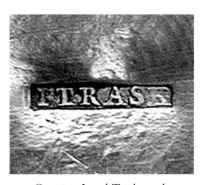

Fake Israel Trask mark   Genuine Israel Trask mark

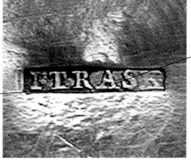

Note: outline of fake mark is too far from letters

Note: different shape on right foot of "R"

Serifs on letters in genuine mark are more pronounced

Flared-Base Beakers with a Fake TD&SB Mark

Flared-Base Beakers with a Fake TD&SB Mark

Here are a pair of footed beakers or church cups, 3⅝ inches tall. They have a gently shaped, almost cup-like body with a very simple flared foot. It is this type of beaker that led to the erroneous attribution which states: this style of beaker is often referred to as an unmarked "Boardman church cup".

Unfortuately, the marks on these two beakers are one of several fake *TD&SB* touchmarks (see pages 71, 74, 111, 112, and 192). All attributions of these beakers to the Boardmans are incorrect because they are based on a fake mark.

It is not known who actually made these. They are scarce, but not extremely rare. None of the other examples are marked. Only these two are known to be marked, and the marks are not legitimate.

Incorrect TD&SB mark

Genuine TD&SB mark

The distance of the letters to the border is greater in the fake mark

Note; the ampersand is crude and blocky as compared to the genuine mark

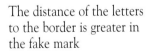

Note: the field behind the letters is deeper in the genuine mark

Tall Beaker with a Modern Danforth Mark

Tall Beaker with a Modern Danforth Mark

This is a tall beaker precisely 5 inches in height, with a top diameter of 3⁹/₁₆ inches, and a bottom diameter of 2⁹/₁₆ inches. The quality of the metal is good. There is some oxide both inside and outside with some signs of wear.

If one looks at the mark on the outside bottom, it has the word *DANFORTH* in a shield-shaped device, but it is the mark of a Danforth working in Connecticut during the mid-20th century. The mark is in-cameo and the lettering is in-cameo. When letters are "in-cameo", they stand in relief as a cameo does. When lettering is intaglio, the letters are cut in so they are actually below the surface. Also, the lettering on this piece looks mechanical and lacks serifs (horizontal extensions at the top and bottom of the character) as one would find on a genuine Danforth touchmark.

This beaker is very high quality and could fool many people into thinking this was an undiscovered Danforth mark. The piece is quite authentic in appearance and metal quality.

Note: the letters in this fake mark appear machine-made and lack the serifs found on genuine Danforth marks

Correct Hamlin Beaker with a Fake
Boardman & Co. Mark

The fake touchmark is struck on the inside bottom
of the beaker, while genuine 3 inch Boardman &
Co. beakers are marked on the outside bottom

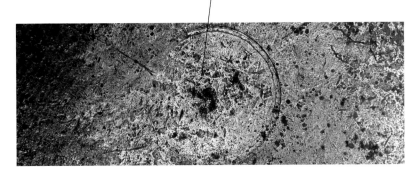

Correct Hamlin Beaker with a Fake Boardman & Co. Mark

This beaker or tumbler is 3¼ inches in height, with a top diameter of 3 inches, and a bottom diameter of approximately 2¼ inches. This is a beaker made by and actually marked by Samuel Hamlin, probably Jr. The mark is one of those very tiny marks on the lip of the beaker (refer to the Hamlin beaker on page 72 which also has a remnant of the small Hamlin mark in a rectangle at the upper lip of the object). In this particular case it is well worn, but once found, you can read the first two letters "HA" very clearly. On the inside bottom of this beaker, a faker has struck a fake *BOARDMAN & C⁰ NEW YORK* eagle mark. It has been struck poorly.

The object was for sale as a Boardman beaker because the faker did not realize that there was a little Hamlin mark on it. Actually, it has far more value as a Hamlin beaker than it would have had as a Boardman piece. But, it is a great teaching tool because the Boardman mark is in an inappropriate place on the inside bottom of the beaker. It is a case where the mark is almost always struck at a poor angle so it is not easily identifiable. The location of the mark also shows the faker had no idea where to place the mark.

Note the position of the
genuine Hamlin touchmark
near the lip of the beaker

Measures

Fake Scottish Glasgow Measure

Fake Scottish Glasgow Measure

This lidded, gill Scottish Glasgow single-dome style measure has a good, albeit, buffed body and handle. However, the hinge, thumbpiece and lid are very crude. A heavy single casting was made to replace a lost lid. The maker probably did not have a complete lid, hinge, and thumbpiece and had to improvise by putting an Edinburgh-style, shell thumbpiece on a Glasgow-style lid. The casting of the medallion on the top is so poorly defined that one cannot tell what it is supposed to be. The type of metal is incorrect, the density of the metal is incorrect, and the style of the thumbpiece is incorrect.

This piece may be the work of an uninformed restorer. The person may have been unaware of the "parts" he was using and not familiar with the appropriate ones, thus creating a fake.

Note: thumbpiece and handle are crudely soldered to a reproduced lid

Fabricated British Baluster Measure with
a Fake Roswell Gleason Mark

Fabricated British Baluster Measure with a Fake Roswell Gleason Mark

This is a British baluster form measure of the double volute type, probably half-pint in capacity, 4 inches tall, with an upper diameter of about 2½ inches. The handle on it is a replacement that probably came from a 20th century English mug, or some other object totally foreign to a measure. The type of metal and handle attachment are inappropriate for this form.

This 18th century body also bears a fake mark of Roswell Gleason on the outside bottom. In addition, there is a large *M* or inverted *W* just to the left of the handle, the origin of which is unknown.

Fake Roswell Gleason mark

Genuine Roswell Gleason mark

Note: background is "muddy" and very uneven

Note: background of genuine mark is smooth and clean

Serifs are heavy and letters of fake mark do not follow a common baseline

Letters are uniform and size is consistent

Fake One-Pint Irish Haystack Measure

This one-pint Irish haystack or harvester style measure is 5¾ inches in height and has no capacity or excise marks. It was turned on a lathe and is a fairly well made fake. One of the primary giveaways is the fact that the lower handle junction is soldered on top of the fillet and not against the body. As a result, light can be seen between the lower part of the handle and the body. When one turns the measure upside down. one observes a whole series of crude, fake marks (e.g. a crowned *X*, a *WM*, an *E*, some hallmarks, and the word *ENGLAND*). It is important to note that the use of the word England, or any other country, was required by the McKinley Act of 1890 to show the country of origin.

Fake One-Pint Irish Haystack Measure

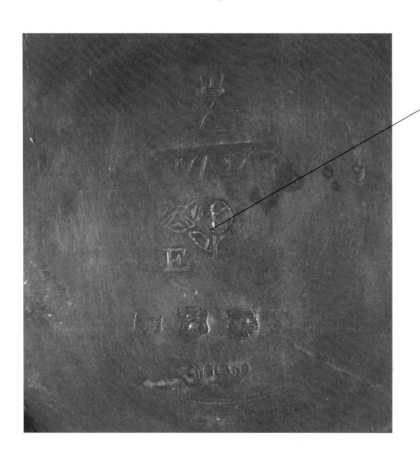

Touch marks are crude and not well defined

Separation of the lower handle from the body is a key indication of a fake

Fake Half-Gill Irish Baluster Measure

Fake Half-Gill Irish Baluster Measure

This half-gill, baluster shaped, open, handleless Irish measure is 2½ inches high with a bottom diameter of 1⅞ and a top diameter of 1⅞ inches. It has artificially created oxide over the entire piece including the bottom. It also has two fake excise marks on the upper rim (i.e. *1 WR 22X* – found on the Richard Neate touchplate[1]).

This item is a product of an early 20th century faker, possibly Neate. These fake measures are dangerous because, even when they are in fine condition, they are not very valuable. Consequently, people do not look at them with a critical eye and can very easily be deceived.

Pitting and surface discoloration on this piece indicate artificial oxide

This is a known fake Irish verification mark by Richard Neate[1]

Reference

1. *The Richard Neate Touch Plate and two others of unknown origin*: The Pewter Society, Welshpool Printing Company, Welshpool, Powys, UK, 1996, p. 7.

Fabricated Half-Gill Lidded Baluster Measure

This half-gill lidded baluster measure with a bud style thumbpiece has a height to the lip of 2⅝ inches and a base diameter of 1¹⁄₁₆ inches.

The body of the measure, and perhaps the handle, appear to be original, but the lid and the thumbpiece are new. The handle seems to be burnt on, and one can see the linen mark on the inside. Because the mold was not secure against the body, there is some flashing on the outside where the pour flowed beyond the sides. This may be a very extensively restored item. The lid is too thin in comparison to the proper lids for this type of measure. If one looks carefully, the detail on the thumbpiece is totally lacking. The edges of the ears have been filed, but the thumbpiece itself is very flat on the back.

Collectors should be aware that just because there is a lid on a measure, it does not mean it was original to the piece.

Fabricated Half-Gill Lidded Baluster Measure

Note: details in the thumbpiece have been filed-in as opposed to cast-in on a genuine Baluster measure

Fake Scottish Tappit Hen Measure

Fake Scottish Tappit Hen Measure

This fake Scottish Tappit Hen measure has a base diameter of 5¹/₁₆ inches, a height to the lip of 9¹/₈ inches and an overall height to the top of the thumb rest of 10³/₄ inches. The metal is far too thin and the handle is a simple strap, soldered against the top of the piece and against the inward curve of the mid-section. The measure has extremely crude, fake marks and a poorly applied *LONDON* in a scroll. It also has a cloven hoof, one of the fake cloven marks of the Birmingham area pewterers. The thumbpiece is nothing more than a simplified S-shape.

In this particular case, the overall weight is the most important part of this fake. It can also be seen how the handle was treated with acid and then colored over as a final aging technique.

Unlike a genuine measure, marks on this fake are flat and not well defined

Note: handle of fake is thin and weak at the junction with the body

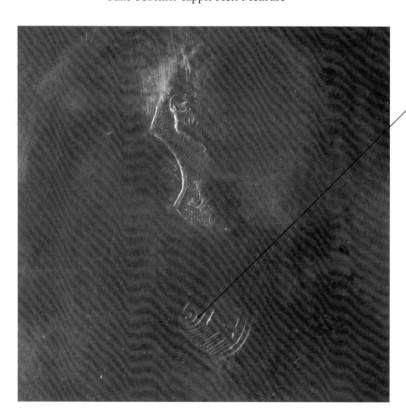

Scottish Half-Pint Measure with a Replaced Lid

Scottish Half-Pint Measure with a Replaced Lid

This Scottish measure has a very heavy casting of a flat lid with an anti-wobble ring inside, and a crude Edinburgh-type thumbpiece. The lid is not at all accurate.

The body of the measure, however, is absolutely right. It is labeled as a half-pint. It has a *VR* mark with an excise mark from Ayrshire and the initials *RG* (probably Robert Galbraith, a maker from Glasgow) on the back of the handle. The handle is from a Scottish measure and could very well be the original handle of this piece. However, it has been removed and then re-soldered, both at the top and bottom, in order to make the fake lid fit. One can observe that the handle is in a slightly different position from its original location.

Note: handle has been re-soldered at the top and bottom

Fake Gill Capacity Irish Haystack Measure

Fake Gill Capacity Irish Haystack Measure

This appears to be an Irish haystack or harvester gill capacity measure. The height to the lip is 3³/₄ inches, with a bottom diameter of 2³/₈ inches.

This measure has no capacity mark on the body, which frequently is an indication of a fake haystack measure. The handle is soldered so that the portion that extends below the band around the middle of the belly stands away from the body. The handle should always be soldered tight against the body. This is another indication of authenticity.

The measure bears the 99 excise mark around the rim and a small *X* and crown on the outside bottom, both of which are shown on the Richard Neate touchplate.[2]

Many beginning collectors are fooled by these marks

Separation of the lower handle from the body is a key indication of a fake

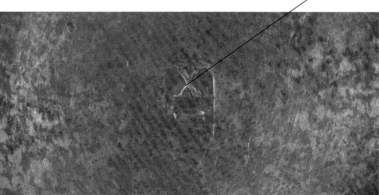

Reference

2. *The Richard Neate Touch Plate and two others of unknown origin*, p. 7.

Irish Haystack Measure with a Fake Austen & Son Cork Mark

Irish Haystack Measure with a Fake Austen & Son Cork Mark

This appears to be an Irish haystack or harvester measure, gill capacity, 3¾ inches in height, and a 2⅜ inch bottom diameter. The piece has a fake *AUSTEN & SON CORK* mark on the outside bottom with the North Main Street address mark. It lacks any capacity mark and has no excise marks on it at all. The handle is soldered to the body in such a way that the lower end of the handle does not fit tightly against the body of the measure, but rests on the rim around the widest portion of the body. This poor fit is inappropriate and is almost always an indication of a fake.

Fake Austen & Son Cork mark   Genuine Austen & Son Cork mark

Note: letters of fake mark are heavy and flat in appearance

Letters of genuine mark are sharp and well defined

Separation of the lower handle from the body is a key indication of a fake

Note: tail of lion in fake mark is much too wide

Fake Swiss Bauchkanne Measures

Fake Swiss Bauchkanne Measures

These are graduated measures of a type known as a Swiss Bauchkanne. The first measure has an overall height of 4¾ inches and the second has an overall height of 5½ inches, both measured to the top of the twin acorn thumbpieces. Each one has an identical angel mark on the lid with what appears to be the initials *BMD*. There does not appear to be any mark indicating where the pieces were made, which suggests that they were imported into this country sometime after World War I. They are not particularly well done as fakes, but have reasonably good artificial color.

Note: mark looks crude and initials are hard to read

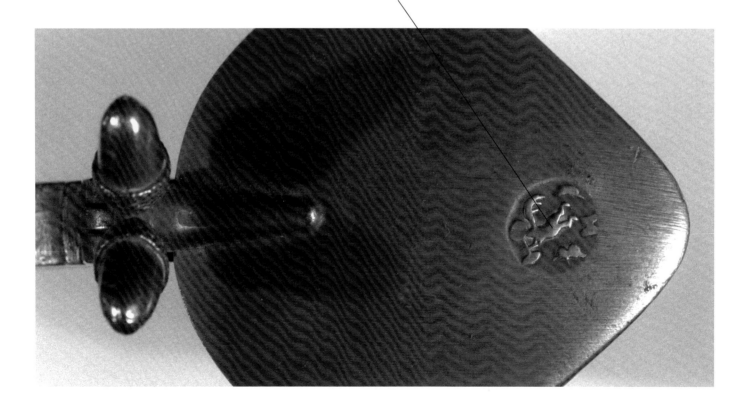

Reproduction Normandy-Type Measure with a Fake Mark

This small, lidded Normandy-type Measure/Flagon has a French twin acorn thumbpiece and a vague heart-shaped lid. The overall height of the piece is 27/8 inches to the top of the thumbpiece. It has a crude, fake mark on the outside bottom that is obviously not old. The piece is made with very leady material. There is not much distress on this item, and the artificial color was probably created by using an acid solution.

Reproduction Normandy-Type Measure with a Fake Mark

The touchmark is very crude and amateurish

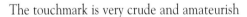

Swiss-Style Wine Measure with Fake Marks

This small, Swiss-style wine measure or flagon is 6 inches tall, has a strap handle, a double-acorn thumbpiece, and a vague heart-shaped lid. On one side is a fake mark of Wallis Canton (a shield with stars inside of it). On the other side is the mark *HB* over a heart enclosed in a dotted circle. These marks are fake.

If one looks on the inside, it is obvious that the handle is soldered on, not burnt on as it should be. The bottom is unfinished and the parting lines of the mold can be seen on the inside of the body. Those parting lines would probably have been machined off if this were produced by a early pewterer. This piece was made in the early 20th century.

Swiss-Style Wine Measure with Fake Marks

Note: handle has been soldered on

Fake marks are bulky and crude

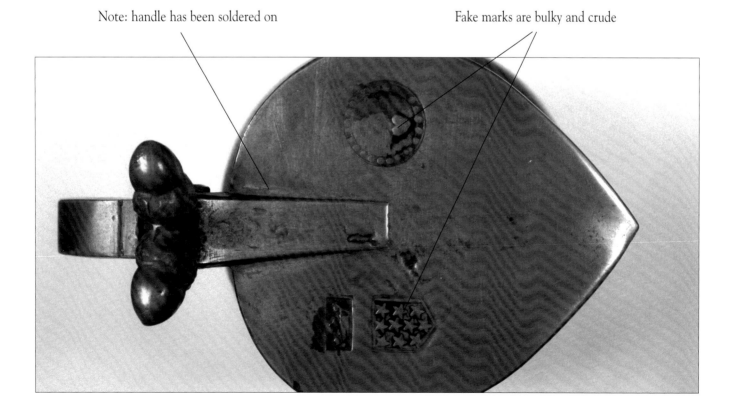

Porringers

Reproduction Crescent Handle Porringer

Reproduction Crescent Handle Porringer

This porringer has a large heart and crescent handle. The bowl diameter is a little short of 4¼ inches and is out of shape. It is a copy of a 19th century porringer type that is fairly well known and never marked.

The bowl on this porringer is spun. In this case, the handle appears to have been cast with the bracket and then sweat soldered to the bowl. There are some repairs to the bowl, it has considerable color and it appears to have been buffed at one time.

This porringer was probably made in the early 20th century and may not have originally been intended to deceive.

Note: sweat soldered joint on bracket

Fake Dolphin Handle Porringer

Fake Dolphin Handle Porringer

This is a dolphin handle porringer with a bowl diameter of 5⅛ inches. The porringer shows considerable wear and tear. There are repairs near the handle and repairs to the side of the bowl. The bowl is spun metal, probably made between 1900 and 1910. The handle is sand cast, copied from the Danforth family example. In this case, the bracket is sand cast separately from the handle and bears no relationship to the bracket on a real dolphin handle porringer. Both the handle and bracket have been sweat soldered to a spun body. There is a lot of scale and considerable color, which might make the novice collector believe this is a legitimate antique porringer.

Another item that should be noted about this particular dolphin handle porringer: while there may have been some British examples where the dolphin handle is found on a bellied style bowl, in America all dolphin handles are found on basin styled bowls.

Note: dolphin scales poorly defined – scales on genuine porringer are sharper

"Blip" on right side of shield also present on genuine Danforth Dolphin handle porringers

Note: sweat soldered joint on bracket

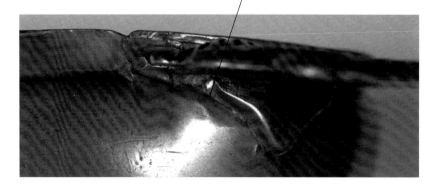

Reproduction Old English Handle Porringer

Reproduction Old English Handle Porringer

This porringer has a diameter of about 3¼ inches. It has an Old English style handle. In this case, the handle and the bracket are cast together then soldered onto a spun bowl. The flared, upper edge of the porringer bowl is actually the product of the metal being folded over. This makes the flared edge thicker.

This piece has a great deal of oxide, a lot of color, and could conceivably fool a new or inexperienced collector. In reality, it is a reproduction from the early 20th century.

Dark oxide gives heavy lead-like appearance

Note: sweat soldered joint on bracket

Porringer with a Fake English Mark

Porringer with a Fake English Mark

This porringer with a basin style bowl is 4¼ inches in diameter. There is a very definite raised ring foot on the bottom. The handle has a strange geometric pattern which could be considered a variation of the old English style. In addition, the handle is soldered up against the side of the bowl with no bracket beneath. The handle is not burnt on in the normal fashion and bears a fake mark of Phillip White – attributed to Richard Neate.

Handle is sweat soldered on to bowl with no bracket

Correct Crescent Handle Porringer with a Fake T.D.B. Mark

Correct Crescent Handle Porringer with a Fake T.D.B. Mark

This is a bellied porringer with a 3¼ inch bowl diameter. The porringer and handle are definitely American, but it bears a fake *T.D.B.* (Thomas Danforth Boardman) eagle in a dotted waisted oval on the upper surface of the handle. The mark is the same fake mark as on the correct flower handle porringer illustrated on page 117. This fake *T.D.B.* eagle mark is one of two that appear in this book (see pages 117 and 164).

In addition, this mark is often found on 8 inch to 9 inch plates. Frequently the plate is legitimate, but the mark is wrong.

Fake T.D.B. mark   Genuine T.D.B. mark

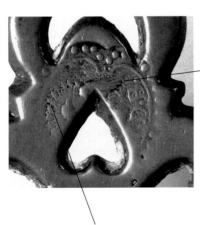

Note: stars are heavier than on genuine mark

Fake mark is struck sideways

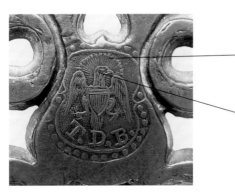

Stars are smaller on genuine mark

Head of eagle is an outline and more defined in correct mark

Reproduction Crescent Handle Porringer

This porringer has a basin style bowl, $2^7/_8$ inches in diameter, with a heart and crescent handle. This is a crude and leady reproduction. It appears to be cast all in one piece (handle and bowl together). There is no definition on the back where a bracket would be, and no linen mark.

This item has also been found made of iron and brass. The iron, brass and pewter porringers were cast in sand using the same pattern for all.

Reproduction Crescent Handle Porringer

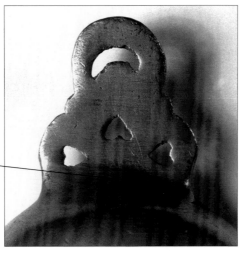

Handle is narrower and crudely finished on reproduction

Handle and bowl are cast as one piece

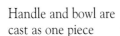

Crude Flowered Handle Porringers with Fake Marks

Crude Flowered Handle Porringers with Fake Marks

These two porringers are from the same mold. One has a fake American mark and one has a fake English mark. The porringers have a crude bowl, 5¼ inches in diameter with a definite ring foot on the bottom. The handles are identical and are sometimes referred to as flowered handle porringers. However, these are unrefined and incorrect representations of that form.

One of the porringers bears a rather contemporary, yet simplistic looking mark of *P. BOYD. PHIL*[A] in a serrated outline on the outside bottom. It is one of those marks which Laughlin illustrated in his first volume. He indicated pieces with this mark had been made in Europe for sale in New York City department stores.

The other identical porringer has a fake mark of *TS* (Thomas Smith), with a bell suspended from a heart, and the word *LONDON* in a separate die. The accumulated wear and distress to the surface makes these dangerous. These porringers were probably made between 1910 and 1920.

Fake Parks Boyd mark

Fake Thomas Smith mark

Eagle looks mechanically produced, lacks detail and looks flat

Sans serif letters on fake mark look machine made

Note: fine sawtooth border on genuine mark

Eagle is detailed and has more depth

Letters look hand-cut, have serifs and vary in width

Genuine Parks Boyd mark

"Bow Tie"
half apertures

Fake Flowered Handle Porringer

The diameter of this porringer is 4¹/₄ inches. It is a very exaggerated bowl, spun, with the flared collar of the bowl made from a separate piece which was soldered on. One can clearly see the solder where the collar was joined to the bowl, and where the ring is joined together in front of the handle. This is a very poor attempt at a fake or reproduction. There are no marks on this piece. It has a flowered handle similar to some unmarked Rhode Island examples, including "bow tie" style half apertures at the lower part of the handle.

This porringer also has a separately cast bracket, and the bracket and the handle are sweat soldered inappropriately to the body of the porringer. The handle is much thicker than the handle of a legitimate period porringer.

Fake Flowered Handle Porringer

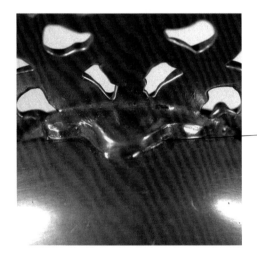

Note: sweat soldered
joint on bracket

Handle is sweat soldered
to body and is overly thick

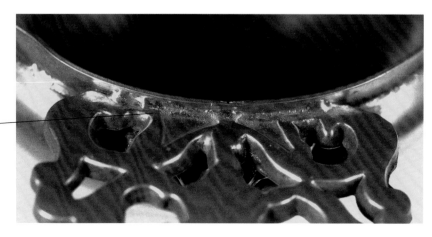

Crown Handle Porringer with a False Josiah Danforth Mark

Crown Handle Porringer with a False Josiah Danforth Mark

This is a porringer with a bellied bowl 5³/₁₆ inches in diameter. It has a crown handle with a wide tapered spline on the back. This piece bears the eagle mark of Josiah Danforth of Middletown, Connecticut on the face of the handle. However, the mark is cast in, rather than struck.

On the back of the bowl is the mark "Stieff Pewter, Old Sturbridge Village (OSV)" with their cricket symbol. The bowl is spun and the handle is sweat soldered on. With a little bit of work, one could remove the Stieff Pewter, Old Sturbridge Village marks and make it into a successful fake.

Note: position of eagle on all of these Stieff "Danforth" porringers is exactly the same

Fake Josiah Danforth mark

Star in fake touchmark looks more like a bead – stars in genuine mark are well defined

Casting flaws left a void in the touchmark

Genuine Josiah Danforth mark

Stieff Pewter mark

Fake Crown Handle Porringer

This is a porringer with a bellied bowl having a top diameter of 4½ inches and a very crude crown handle. The bowl is spun, not cast. If one looks closely at where the handle is attached to the inside of the bowl, you can see the stress lines caused by the spinning process. The handle is very crude, both front and back, and inappropriately sweat soldered to the body of the porringer.

The color is quite dark and may have been artificially induced to give an antique appearance.

Fake Crown Handle Porringer

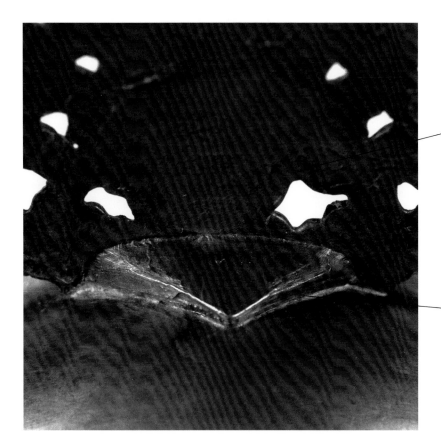

Back of handle is crude and unplanished

Note: sweat soldered joint on bracket

Tab Handle Porringers with Modern Marks

Tab Handle Porringers with Modern Marks

These are two Pennsylvania tab handle porringers having a bowl diameter of 5¼ inches. The mold for these porringers was made using a period porringer for a pattern. The handle is solid cast as one piece with the bowl, as were the originals. Both of these porringers are identical. Every nick and scratch is the same. One porringer bears the mark of J. Thomas Stauffer. The Eagle mark is resting on an oval with the initials *JTS*. The other porringer had the same mark and it was purposely removed. This process probably took about 20 minutes.

If this was an attempt to actually fake this piece, one would spend more time and it would be very difficult to tell what had been done. So, even though Mr. Stauffer has placed his mark on the back, this demonstrates how easy it would be to take the mark off and make it into a salable "antique" porringer.

Touchmark by J. Thomas Stauffer closely resembles Eagle touchmarks by period pewterers

Touchmark removed

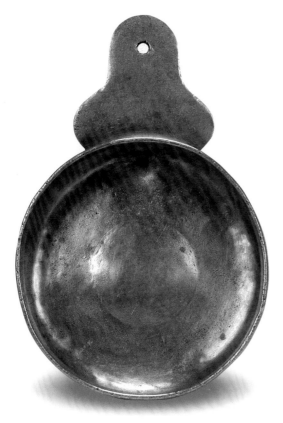

Fake Rhode Island Tab Handle Porringer

This porringer has a bellied bowl with an upper diameter of 5 inches. It has a Rhode Island solid handle in the trefoil design. The bowl of this porringer, although very heavy, is spun. The upper lip of the bowl is formed by flipping the metal over on top of itself. One can see where the soldering is incomplete. The handle was probably copied from a legitimate Rhode Island porringer.

There has also been some attempt to mechanically distress this piece.

Fake Rhode Island Tab Handle Porringer

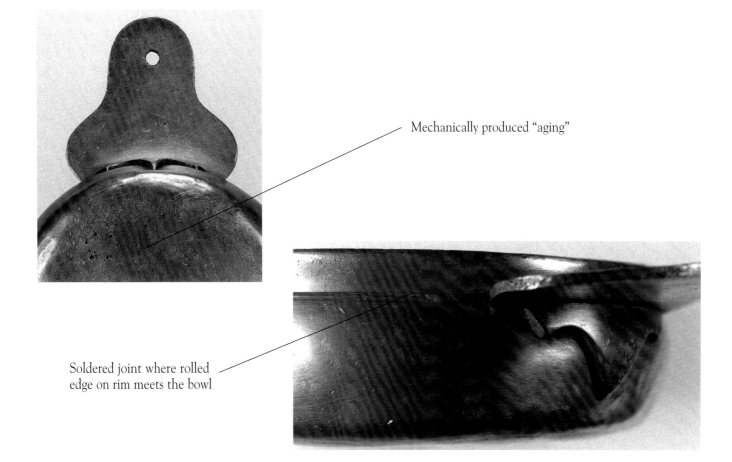

Mechanically produced "aging"

Soldered joint where rolled edge on rim meets the bowl

Correct Tab Handle Porringer with a Fake Richard Lee Mark

Correct Tab Handle Porringer with a Fake Richard Lee Mark

This is a bellied bowl porringer with a top diameter of 5⁷/₁₆ inches and a solid trefoil handle. This is a correct Rhode Island, 18th century porringer in every way, made by either the Melvilles or the Belchers.

Unfortunately, there is a fake L413 *RICHARD•LEE* mark on the upper surface of the handle (see p. 73). This mark is found on a variety of porringers and plates of styles not associated with any Lee touchmark.

Fake Richard Lee mark   Genuine Richard Lee mark

Fake mark has more distance between letters and edge

Note: fake mark has fine, evenly spaced serrations on the sawtooth edge

Letters on genuine mark are irregular and appear hand-cut

Reproduction Flowered Handle Porringer

Reproduction Flowered Handle Porringer

The top diameter of the bowl of this small porringer is 2 inches. The handle is a variation of the flowered handle. It is very similar to a style made by Richard Lee, but this is a spun, bellied bowl versus a cast, basin bowl. The handle has no bracket and is soldered directly onto the bowl. On the bottom is the mark of William Cowlishaw, a Boston pewterer, who worked from 1898 to 1933. This is his later mark, probably used somewhere between 1920 and 1930.

This is not a fake, just a reproduction piece made by Cowlishaw. Many reproduction porringers have handles derived or copied from period handles.

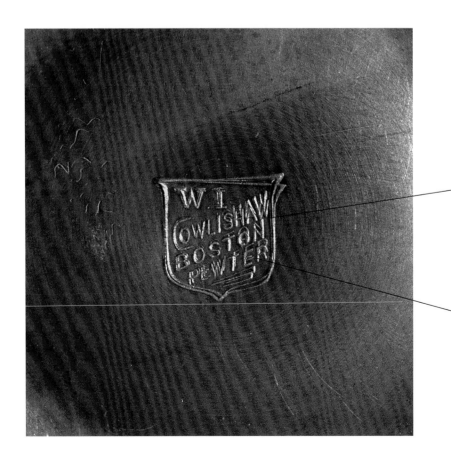

Note: slanted lettering in mark looks thin and too contemporary

Period touchmarks do not use the word "pewter" in the mark

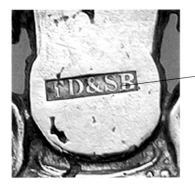

Spun Crown Handle Porringer with a Fake TD&SB Mark

Spun Crown Handle Porringer with a Fake TD&SB Mark

The upper bowl diameter of this porringer is 5³/₁₆ inches. The handle and the bracket were cast separately and sweat soldered to a spun bowl. The handle is a direct copy casting of a real Boardman handle with the *TD&SB* mark in it (see other false marks on pages 71, 74, 78, 112, and 192). This handle, copied from an original Boardman porringer, has the *TD&SB* mark "upside down", as it is typically found. For whatever reason, the Boardmans apparently thought this mark on a porringer was more easily read in this position. This porringer was probably made to deceive because the mark is also "upside down."

Incorrect cast TD&SB mark

Genuine struck TD&SB mark

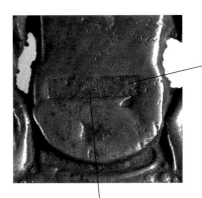

Letters are soft and lack any definition in fake touchmark

Fake mark is almost illegible, but not from wear

Letters in genuine mark are sharp and clear

Correct Crown Handle Porringer with a Fake TD&SB Mark

Correct Crown Handle Porringer with a Fake TD&SB Mark

This is one of those well known American crown handle porringers with a very exaggerated belly to the bowl.

This is an honest porringer with a fake *TD&SB* mark struck on it (see other false marks on pages 71, 74, 78, 111, and 192). Also note that the fake mark is not "upside down" as genuine *TD&SB* marks were usually struck on crown handles.

These particular crown handle porringers are fairly common, and the weight and type of workmanship indicate they were probably made in New England during the first quarter of the 19th century.

Fake TD&SB mark

Genuine TD&SB mark

Note: distance from letters to edge is greater in fake mark

Letters are spaced further apart in fake mark

Crude, soldered repair to handle joint

Fake Dolphin Handle Porringer

Fake Dolphin Handle Porringer

The upper diameter of the basin on this porringer is 5⅝ inches. This is a dolphin handle porringer, but not from the Danforth mold. It is another American mold where bubbles come out of the dolphin's mouth. The entire porringer is a fabrication – the bowl, the handle, as well as the bracket. However, it was made in an appropriate style and it appears as though the handle was burnt on. In fact, it was sweat soldered at the two sides (extremes) of the handle. That leaves the impression it might have been burnt on, but it wasn't. The back of the handle and bracket are inappropriately finished. The initials *MK*, in a fairly modern die, were struck into the back of the handle.

This piece has a handle cast in a mold made from a genuine Dolphin handle porringer, but it is a badly constructed fake.

Lip is squared-off with more overhang than is normal on a period porringer

Sweat soldered on edges of handle bracket

Note: there is a gap between handle and bowl as on genuine porringer

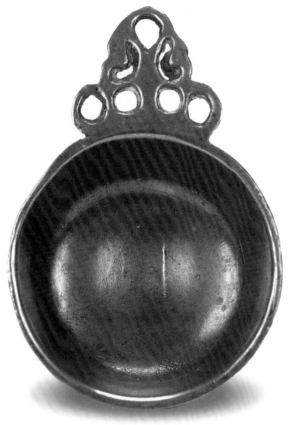

Fake Taster Porringer

Fake Taster Porringer

This taster porringer has a bowl diameter of 2¹/₈ inches. It appears to be identical to one illustrated in a *PCCA Bulletin* article written by Sandy MacFarlane (page 214 of Volume 6). It is obvious looking at the photograph of Mr. MacFarlane's example that it also is a fake. Both of these porringers were cast with the bowl and handle together as one unit. They were made out of metal with a high lead content and have casting faults, a feature that would not be present on a genuine period porringer.

This porringer was most likely made sometime in the early 20th century.

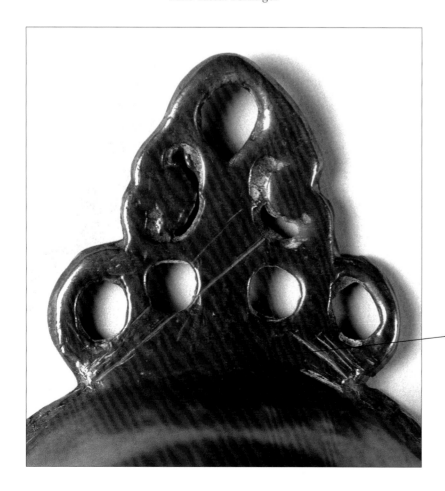

Sweat soldered on edges of handle bracket

Fake British Porringer with a Shell Handle

This basin style porringer, with a bowl diameter of precisely 3 inches and a shell-like handle, was cast as a single unit. This porringer bears an *X* mark with a crown above it. It shows some light oxide formation, but is definitely of modern manufacture. The acid treatment and artificial distressing on the back were probably done in the early 20th century.

Fake British Porringer with a Shell Handle

Shell handle and bowl have been cast as one piece

Fake Two-Handle Porringer by Richard Neate

Fake Two-Handle Porringer by Richard Neate

The diameter of this two-handle porringer is 3³/₈ inches. It has very short, tab-type solid handles with a less than one half inch protrusion from each side. This piece is in the form of a Scottish quaich. On the bottom are initials believed to be those of Richard Neate – in this case shown as *N.R.* This initial hallmark is above two other hallmarks, one depicting a rooster and the other the head of a griffin. Both images are within a shield-like device.

This is another of the Richard Neate British fakes made in the early 20th century.

The reversed initials N.R are frequently referred to as "Naughty Richard"

Correct Flowered Handle Porringer with a Fake T.D.B. Mark

Correct Flowered Handle Porringer with a Fake Thomas Danforth Boardman Mark

This is a 5½ inch flowered handle porringer with a "bow tie" design at the lower portion of the handle. This is a genuine period porringer. However, it has a fake Thomas Danforth Boardman, beaded eagle touchmark struck on the face side of the handle. This fake *T.D.B.* eagle mark is one of two that appear in this book (see pages 101 and 164). While this is the appropriate manner for striking this particular mark, the die is false, and therefore it was an attempt by someone to deceive.

The die for the mark on this porringer is particularly well executed. If compared to a hand-drawn touchmark, one might believe it to be correct.

Fake T.D.B. mark

Genuine T.D.B. mark

Initials are too close together on fake mark

Beads in border are smaller and spaced further apart

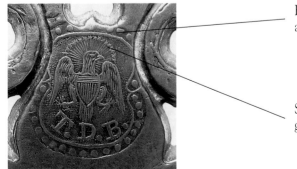

Beading is larger and fills the border

Stars are finer in genuine mark

Flowered Handle Porringer with a Fake Samuel E. Hamlin Mark

Flowered Handle Porringer with a Fake Samuel E. Hamlin Mark

This is a 5⅜ inch flowered handle porringer. It has a misshapen bracket that is very undefined. The handle is not well finished and bears a fake touchmark of Samuel E. Hamlin. The Hamlins, both Sr. and Jr., are well known for careful finishing of porringer handles.

This fake touchmark has also been found on crown handle porringers, a style not made by the Hamlins.

Fake Samuel Hamlin mark

Genuine Samuel Hamlin mark

Note: eagle is more diminutive and beak is further away from the banner in fake mark

Ring on anchor is small compared to larger ring on genuine mark

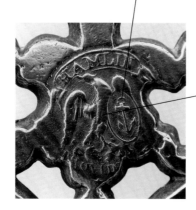

Eagle is wider and more robust in genuine mark – beak touches banner

Spoons & Ladles

Fake John Bassett Spoons

Fake John Bassett Spoons

These are round-bowled, rather small tablespoons, 6⅜ inches in length, with a chicken's claw support underneath the bowl. Any and all spoons with such a support under the bowl are fakes. Both of these spoons have a cast *IB* mark on the face of the spoon (*I* was used for both the initial *I* and *J* during the 17th and 18th centuries). They were intended to be sold as John Bassett spoons.

These spoons are part of a larger set which are all fakes. They were probably made around 1900. One can see that every little nick and scratch is duplicated in each spoon, indicating that all were cast from the same mold. There are a few dents in one that do not appear in the others. That may be from use. But, if one looks at the bowl straight on, there's a little nick to the left of the handle join. That nick is in exactly the same place on all the spoons. The major pit marks in the bottom of the bowl are the same and are in exactly the same place.

Although this is a fake mark, it is important to note that "I" was used for both the initial I and J in the 17th and 18th centuries

Fake Richard Lee Spoon

This is a teaspoon, 5½ inches in length with a pointed bowl and a stylized shell drop on the back of the handle. It is reminiscent of many American Britannia spoons made from the 1850s through the 1870s in several Connecticut shops. The spoon has the fake L413 *RICHARD • LEE* mark on it and was probably made some 40 or 50 years after Richard Lee had died (see p. 73).

Fake Richard Lee Spoon

Fake Richard Lee mark

Genuine Richard Lee mark

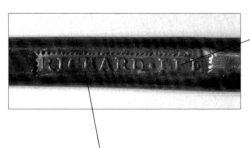

Fake mark has more distance between letters and edge

Note: fake mark has fine, evenly spaced serrations on the sawtooth edge

Letters on genuine mark are irregular and appear hand-cut

Fake Joseph Belcher Spoon

Fake Joseph Belcher Spoon

This is a tablespoon, 8 inches in length, with an elongated oval bowl and no drop or support where the bowl and the handle join. It has cast decoration on the back of the handle consisting of a vase of flowers, along with a shield and other devices. It also has a fake, oval *J:B* mark, (a spurious copy of the mark of Joseph Belcher) struck into the shield portion of the decoration.

If this fake mark were to appear on a genuine Belcher spoon, it would certainly fool many collectors, particularly if they were using a reference book with line drawings of marks rather than photos. Using a book with strong, clear photographs is always preferred.

Fake Joseph Belcher mark

Genuine Joseph Belcher mark

Note: too much space between the letters and the border

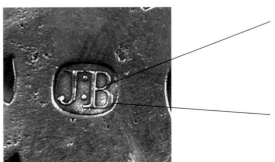

Note: thin serifs and cross bars on letters of genuine mark

Space between letters and border is very close

20th Century Spoon with Fake Paul Revere Mark

This is a tablespoon, 7¹/₂ inches long. The bowl is egg-shaped with a broad tapering flat handle. On the back is the rather well known *P.R* mark which has been attributed over the years to Paul Revere. But, this spoon was made in the 20th century. Paul Revere never made pewter.

20th Century Spoon with Fake Paul Revere Mark

Note: letters lack serifs and look very crude

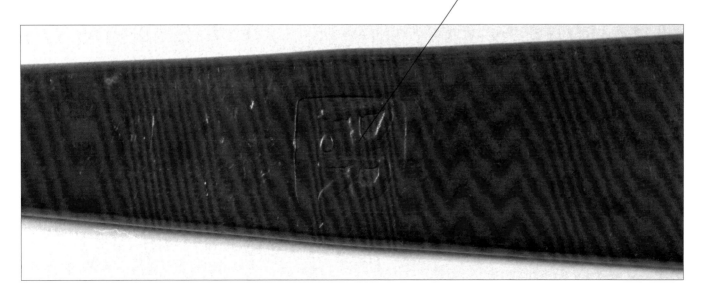

Reproduction Spoons

Reproduction Spoons

The first spoon (far left) is a round-bowled spoon, generally of the Jamestown, Virginia type. It has the mark of William Kayhoe, one of the late Presidents of the PCCA. The spoon is marked *KAYHOE RICHMOND*, with another device in the middle. It was something Mr. Kayhoe made, not intending to fool anyone. However, if this spoon was distressed severely, his mark removed, treated with acid, and buried in the ground, 10 or 20 years from now someone might consider it an antique.

The second spoon is also a round-bowled spoon of an early Virginia form. This is a crude copy of the Joseph Copeland spoon, marked *JOSEPH COPELAND CHUCKATUCK 1675*. This spoon was actually made by Stieff Pewter. It is marked as such on the back of the handle and is a late 20th century reproduction.

Reproduction Rat-tail Spoons

These are spoons with fig-shaped bowls and a simplified rat-tail support at the juncture of the handle and bowl. The spoons have long, narrow handles and each one bears a very crude oval mark enclosing a rampant lion, with a dotted outline at one end. The marks are struck so that in some cases you see the front of the lion, and in some cases you see the back of the lion. The spoons also show some coloration which was undoubtedly caused by acid treatment.

These spoons were made in the 20th century with no maker's mark other than a star on the back of each handle.

Reproduction Rat-tail Spoons

Single stars were rarely used as marks

Note: die is crude and lacks detail

Dog-nosed Handle Reproduction Spoons

These are recent spoon castings, probably from an old mold, with a dog-nosed type handle and a long rat-tail support under the oval bowl. This style of spoon was popular from 1690 to 1780, both in North America and in England. However, these examples are reproductions. They were cast in an old mold, finished incorrectly, and were probably made in the latter portion of the 20th century.

Dog-nosed Handle Reproduction Spoons

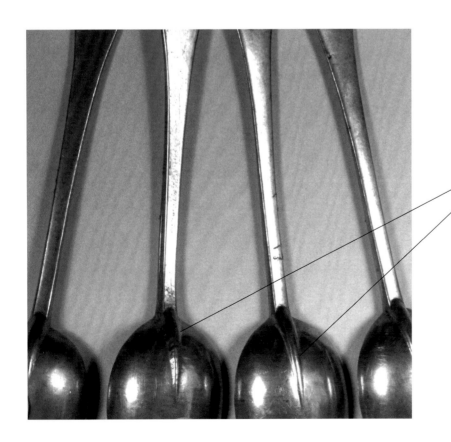

Rat-tail supports are clean and sharp which indicates a recent casting

(Front)   (Back)
Reproduction Ladle

Reproduction Ladle

This is a very charming little sauce or gravy ladle. The bowl is only 1⁷/₁₆ inches wide and not particularly deep. The handle, not including the bowl, is 4¹/₄ inches long. This item is well made, has good metal, and it could easily pass for an 1840 to 1860 sauce ladle.

On the back of the ladle is the old Colonial Williamsburg cypher. This is a very light, incised mark. But, because it is incised, the mark could be easily removed or covered over with a little drop of pewter, then brushed off. That would deceptively make this into an "antique" sauce ladle.

Incised touchmark is a
Colonial Williamsburg cypher

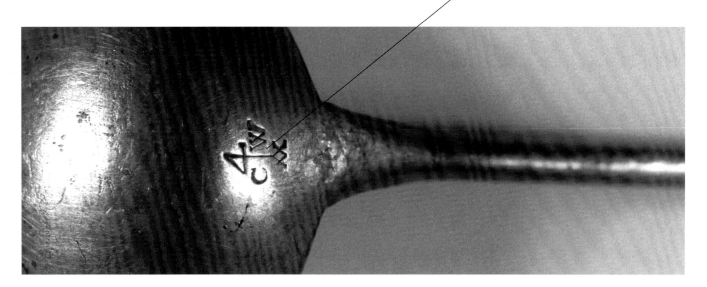

Candlesticks

Reproduction Mid-Drip Candlesticks

Reproduction Mid-Drip Candlesticks

Note: letters lack serifs and appear machine made

This is a pair of baluster-turned, mid-drip candlesticks, 6¾ inches tall with the initials *RN* enclosed in a shield on the upper surface of both drip trays. The style of these candlesticks is frequently referred to as Heemskirk style sticks, so named for Jacob van Heemskirk.

Jacob van Heemskirk was part of an expedition searching for a Northeast passage to China in the 16th century. Heemskirk's party became stranded and although he survived, his camp was buried in the ice and snow along with all of his supplies. Candlesticks of this form were found when the remains of the camp were discovered in 1871.

These candlesticks are reproductions rather than fakes, and they were made in the early 20th century. They are a pair, but there are certain dissimilarities, especially in the area where the shaft joins the base. They are very crudely made. For example, the lines on the edges of the drip trays are cast in and have some areas where the casting is not well done. In the lowest part of the drip tray, there are crude casting marks still evident. On the bottom of the candlestick where the lower shaft joins the base from the underside, the unfinished surface is particularly obvious. Although colored artificially with acid, there are some very sharp, new surfaces.

Unfortunately, with years of use and wear, an unscrupulous dealer or an unknowing collector might well think the candlesticks were antiques.

Reproduction Chamberstick with a Fake Parks Boyd Mark

Reproduction Chamberstick with a Fake Parks Boyd Mark

This is a very crude chamber candlestick or chamberstick with saucer base. It has a very deep saucer with a strange candle socket having no stem, and a crude ring handle. Altogether modern looking in every respect, it bears the mark of Parks Boyd on the outside bottom. This is the same *P. BOYD. PHIL*[A] fake mark found on a porringer on page 103 and the same fake mark that was illustrated by Ledlie I. Laughlin in *Pewter in America, It's Makers and Marks*.

If one looks hard enough along the rim, one will find the tiny word "England". When these pieces were being made and sent to the United States, the U.S. government required that the country of origin be indicated on any imported object. However, because the mark was so small, it was very easy to remove it with just a few swipes of an emery cloth or steel wool.

Fake Parks Boyd mark

Genuine Parks Boyd mark

Eagle looks mechanically produced, lacks detail and looks flat

Sans serif letters on fake mark look machine made

Note: fine sawtooth border on genuine mark

Eagle is detailed and has more depth

Letters look hand-cut, have serifs and vary in width

Genuine Parks Boyd mark

Roswell Gleason Candlestick with a Fabricated Base

This candlestick is 6¼ inches tall. It was made by taking the shaft from a genuine Gleason candlestick and applying the base from an entirely different candlestick or lamp. The seam is just below the section of the original base where the touch is located. The shaft has a center knop with a wafer above and below. The candle socket is attached on top of the shaft. There is a slight remnant of the original base that bears the genuine Roswell Gleason mark.

The first thing one notices is a very unsightly repair to the upper candle socket. A crude replacement has been poorly soldered in its place. That alone would indicate a repaired candlestick. However, if one examines the base, approximately one quarter of an inch below the joint of the shaft and base, another join line becomes apparent. In essence, the shaft has been "married" to the base.

While the touchmark is legitimate, this piece should not be considered a fake. It is, in fact, a bad repair. The addition of the replacement base, along with the replaced bobeche, has so extensively altered this item that it has removed any value as an antique.

Joint

Roswell Gleason Candlestick with a Fabricated Base

Interior seam where two pieces were joined together

Genuine Roswell Gleason mark

Note: "puddled" metal from crude soldering

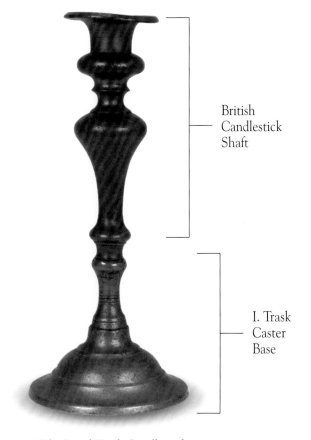

British
Candlestick
Shaft

I. Trask
Caster
Base

Fake Israel Trask Candlestick

Fake Israel Trask Candlestick

This is a married piece. The upper section is a genuine British candlestick from about 1820. It is joined to the base and lower shaft of an Israel Trask caster holder from which the bottle frame and upper handle have been removed. 3¼ inches up from the bottom is a crude and very obvious join line. The candlestick is top heavy because the weight of the upper part of the stick is greater than that of the base. Israel Trask did make larger caster holders and a larger base would have been more appropriate for the faker to have used. Many other pewterers also made caster holders that had larger bases and there are more convincing upper portions of candlesticks that could have been joined onto this Trask base. If done by an expert, such a joining would have been hard to detect.

There is no evidence that Israel Trask ever made candlesticks. He did, however, make lamps using this base. This piece even has a label on the bottom, "Trask, Beverly 1807-1856."

Note: this touchmark is genuine, as is the base on which it was struck – therefore some fakes are made by taking real marked parts from one form and creating totally new ones

Late 19th Century Reproduction Candlestick

This late 19th or early 20th century, small candlestick has a height of 5¹/₈ inches. It is made of a leady grade of pewter. The stick was transformed, during the last quarter of the 20th century, into an electrified candlestick. In addition, the outside bottom may have had some nickel plate at one time.

While the design of this piece is reasonably accurate for an early 19th century candlestick, both the weight and construction are totally inappropriate.

Late 19th Century Reproduction Candlestick

Note: small holes and depressions have been added manually to simulate pitting and wear

Fake Calder Candlestick

This candlestick was made by using the shaft and base of a late European candlestick, and adding the base of a William Calder tea or coffeepot. This created a solid bottom base. The fit of the two elements is very well done and carefully attached. The color of the piece is uniform. All these factors could easily fool a beginning collector.

One needs to study actual period candlesticks made by William Calder and his contemporaries. The fact that this style of candlestick is unlike anything made by these individuals should be a clear warning.

Fake Calder Candlestick

Note: while these three impressions constitute a genuine Calder mark, the style number 13 was used exclusively on teapots and coffeepots

Basins & Bowls

Danforth Basin with a Fake Israel Trask Mark

Danforth Basin with a Fake Israel Trask Mark

The 7¼ inch basin is a unique American size. This size was probably the one referred to in Samuel Danforth's inventories as a wine quart basin. It is slightly smaller than a standard quart basin which is approximately 8 inches in diameter. From what is known, only Samuel Danforth (Hartford, Connecticut) and the Boardmans made this size basin. This piece is a legitimate Samuel Danforth basin with minor repairs. His mark appears on the inside bottom. Unfortunately, the mark is so poorly struck that an individual would have to be familiar with this particular Samuel Danforth touchmark in order to recognize it.

However, on the outside bottom, the basin has a fake *I•TRASK* mark. Someone has scraped away a small flat spot and struck a Trask mark. Not only did Israel Trask not make this size basin, but the mark is a known fake Trask touchmark. Inside the basin, the middle of the faint Samuel Danforth mark has been flattened by the die of the Trask mark struck on the outside bottom.

Fake Israel Trask mark

Genuine Israel Trask mark

Note: outline of fake mark is sharp, with flared corners

Note: different shape on right foot of "R"

Serifs on letters in genuine mark are more pronounced

Fake Wash Bowl with a Correct Roswell Gleason Mark

Genuine Roswell Gleason mark

Fake Wash Bowl with a Correct Roswell Gleason Mark

This appears to be a hanging wash bowl with an attached decorative brass ring. The piece has been constructed from the bottom of a Roswell Gleason water pitcher. A homemade upper section, with an approximate diameter of 11 inches, was added at a later date.

The bottom bears the genuine touchmark of *ROSWELL GLEASON* with a number *2*. This mark is frequently found on water pitchers by this maker.

This piece represents an attempt by someone to create a form which Roswell Gleason never made.

Upper bowl and ring were added later

Note: foot from genuine Roswell Gleason pitcher

Pennsylvania Basin with a Fake Boardman & Co. Mark

Pennsylvania Basin with a Fake Boardman & Co. Mark

This American basin is 6⁹/₁₆ inches in diameter. The form suggests a New York or Pennsylvania origin rather than New England because it is relatively shallow and wide. It bears at least one poor strike of *BOARDMAN & Cᵒ* with *NEW–YORK* and an eagle on the outside bottom. This is not where Boardman would have placed the mark. The basin would have been marked on the inside bottom. The poor mark shows only a few of the letters (*DMA*) and part of the eagle with a small portion of the words *NEW–YORK* underneath. The basin was deliberately struck poorly. It was placed on a flat surface and struck from the other side in order to partly obliterate the image.

Fake Boardman & Co. mark   Genuine Boardman & Co. mark

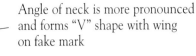

Angle of neck is more pronounced and forms "V" shape with wing on fake mark

Note: stepped angle of wing near neck on genuine mark

Rococo Saucer with a Reproduction Mark

Rococo Saucer with a Reproduction Mark

This is a small, 4¹⁵/₁₆ inch saucer of Rococo design. On the underside is a reproduction touchmark made to look old and struck off center. This piece was cast in a mold, but shows no signs of being hand finished. A period Rococo piece would have burnished surfaces and the edges would have been scraped.

This is most likely a 20th century reproduction not necessarily made to deceive, but sold as a decorative piece.

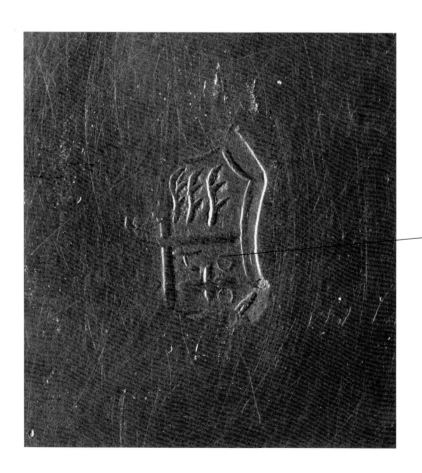

Note: "Coat of Arms" mark is flat and unrefined

Baptismal Style Bowl with a Fake Frederick Bassett Mark

Baptismal Style Bowl with a Fake Frederick Bassett Mark

This footed, open Baptismal style bowl has an upper diameter of 4¼ inches and a base diameter of 2⅞ inches. It was probably made as a nut or ice cream dish. The bowl has a fake Frederick Bassett mark on the outside bottom. This fake mark has a fan-shaped floral device similar to the genuine mark, and is pictured in Ledlie I. Laughlin's *Pewter in America, It's Makers and Marks*, Volume II.

The Bassetts never made a form like this and when the mark is compared to a legitimate Frederick Bassett touchmark, the differences become obvious.

Fake Frederick Bassett mark   Genuine Frederick Bassett mark

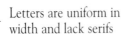

Letters are uniform in width and lack serifs

Note: foliate design is an outline and appears machine made

Letters vary in width and have serifs

Note: "hand-cut" character of die on genuine mark

Reproduction Barber Bowl with Fake Marks

Reproduction Barber Bowl with Fake Marks

This is barber's basin, 10³/₄ inches at the long axis of the oval and 6¹/₂ inches wide to the inside of the cutout on one side of the bowl. The bowl has wriggle-work decoration around the entire face of the flat rim. The surface of the rim was then buffed to make the wrigglework less defined. In fact, the decoration may even have been cast-in as part of the original molding.

There appear to be two attempts at some kind of a mark directly opposite the cutout. There are also two marks on the back of the bowl that depict what appears to be a golden fleece with a crown above it. These are not period touchmarks.

The item is made of a very poor grade of pewter. It is thick and heavy, and essentially unfinished. Along with the wrigglework decoration, there is some sanding over the surface.

Marks are crude and lack definition

Plates & Dishes

20th Century English Saucer with Fake Marks

20th Century English Saucer with Fake Marks

This is a 4¹/₈ inch diameter saucer with a flat rim and bearing, on the back, a fake hallmark of Bush & Perkins, and a Griffin's head, as well as a crowned *X*. This is one of many pieces which were manufactured in the early 20th century and believed to have been made to deceive. It has a great deal of artificial wear all over the surface which is accomplished by tumbling in a machine with pieces of metal or other hard objects. This saucer also has artificial color which was created using acid.

Fake Bush & Perkins hallmarks

Genuine Bush & Perkins hallmarks

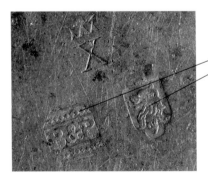

Fake Bush & Perkins hallmarks are crude and lion's head mark is out of position in sequence

Note: authentic Bush & Perkins hallmarks are finely cut with a smaller ampersand between the "B" and "P" in the initial mark

Pair of Fake Saucers with Fake Marks

Pair of Fake Saucers with Fake Marks

These are a pair of flat rim saucers, 4⁷/₁₆ inches in diameter. They each have a fake hallmark on the upper surface with what appears to be a bird with displayed wings. It also has a *GK* or some other combination of initials. There is no sign of any marks on the back. These are cast pieces, with identical faults on each saucer.

These overly large and crude marks do not match any known, legitimate American, English or Continental touchmarks

Reproduction Multi-Reeded Saucers with Fake Marks

Reproduction Multi-Reeded Saucers with Fake Marks

These two saucers are 3⅝ inches in diameter with what one might refer to as a multiple-reed rim. The reeding is actually created by incised lines. There is also a concentric circle turned in the middle of the well of the saucers. Each saucer bears four hallmarks with a rampant lion-in-shield on the upper rim. On the back, each saucer has a struck mark – *S. ORFORD*, in an oval. One has a single *X* mark below the *ORFORD*; the other has two crowned X marks flanking the *ORFORD*. The one with the single *X* mark is also marked "George Inn of Hampton Court".

These saucers were made in great quantity as souvenir items and are still being sold today. They were created sometime between 1890 and 1930, and appear to have the same mark that is illustrated in Cotterell's book, although the lion hallmarks are slightly different.

Letters in mark are blocky
and inconsistent

Note: reeds are incised
rather than molded

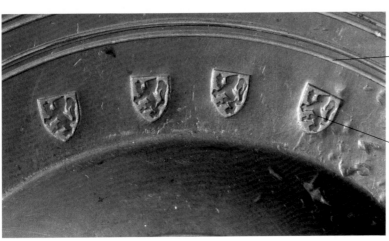

Hallmarks are very large, crude
in appearance and lack detail

20th Century Saucer with a Fake Raised London Mark

20th Century Saucer with a Fake Raised London Mark

This saucer is 4⁹/₁₆ inches in diameter and has a multiple-reed edge that has been created by extensive lathe work. This lathe work makes it appear as if it has a raised multiple-reeded edge. On the front, the great color or "patina" is really false oxide. The back has never been finished and remains as it came out of the mold.

The back also has a *LONDON* mark in a curved rectangle. This mark is cast in relief on the underside along with a double *X* and crown. The *X* is cast intaglio and the crown is cast in-cameo.

This saucer is definitely a 20th century fake. It is the first time that this mark has been recorded utilizing a raised *LONDON* touchmark and a raised crown with a suppressed *X*, all cast in rather than struck.

This raised ring on the bottom has been cast and is not a feature found on period flatware

Note: marks have been cast in position rather than struck

Reproduction Flat Rim Plate with a Fake English Mark

This is a small, flat rim plate or saucer, 6 inches in diameter, that has been cast in a poorly defined mold. There are some oxide eruptions and other faults. It has a fake *LONDON* mark and fake hallmarks, one of which seems to be an attempt to copy either English pewterer Samuel Cox, or Stint Duncomb. All that can be seen is the single letter "S" along with the word *LONDON* in a bar and, a crowned *X* above. This piece appears to be one of those saucers made in the Birmingham, England area between 1890 and 1930.

Reproduction Flat Rim Plate with a Fake English Mark

Note: marks are very faint and not well defined giving the appearance of extensive wear

Counterfeit Plate with a Cast Blakeslee Barnes Mark

Counterfeit Plate with a Cast Blakeslee Barnes Mark

This is a 7¹³/₁₆ inch diameter plate with what is called a "smooth" rim, not a "flat" rim. The plate actually has a concave rim with no reeding on it. This type of rim is similar to many plates made in Pennsylvania by a pewterer using the *LOVE* bird mark. In this case, the plate bears the marks of Blakeslee Barns on the back (the eagle mark with *BB* and the *B BARNES PHILAD*ᴬ mark). This accurate mark, although a little indistinct, is believed to be one of J.T. Stauffer's first production plates, and is an exact copy cast from a legitimate plate.

Mr. Stauffer sold these plates as reproductions. However, the fact that they are exact copies made from original plates has allowed unknowing and unscrupulous individuals to sell these as period pieces. A number of these plates made their way to public auction where "caveat emptor" is the rule. Thus, many examples of this plate, and the two following plates on pages 153 and 154, made their way to collections.

Cast Blakeslee Barnes mark

Struck Blakeslee Barnes mark

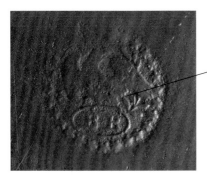

Detail has been lost in the mold-making process with the mark resembling that on a well-worn plate

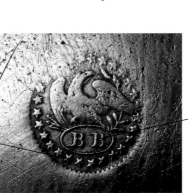

Stars on the struck mark are crisp and well-defined

Note the sharper detail of the oval and initials on a struck mark.

Counterfeit Plates with a Cast Samuel Danforth Mark

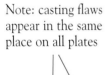

Cast (reproduced) Samuel Danforth mark

Counterfeit Plates with a Cast Samuel Danforth Mark

This set of six 7¹³/₁₆ inch diameter, single-reed plates bear the mark of *SAMUEL DANFORTH* along with his *HARTFORD* mark. They are all absolutely identical. The marks are in exactly the same place, along with every dent and scratch from the original casting.

These are J.T. Stauffer copy castings. Stauffer made molds from a material which could finely cast a human hair. As a result, every knife cut, every pit, and every scratch was reproduced. One will note that on the back of each plate, where the mold might have had some wet spots, little bits of raised matter also caused identical small bumps. All these similarities are a convincing indication that the plates are not legitimate antiques.

Note: casting flaws appear in the same place on all plates

Identical pits and bumps appear on every plate

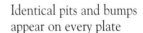

Counterfeit Plates with a Cast Thomas Danforth III Mark

Counterfeit Plates with a Cast Thomas Danforth III Mark

This is one of a pair of single-reed rim plates, 7¹³/₁₆ inches in diameter. They are believed to be the products of J.T. Stauffer. In this particular case, these are two identical plates with a *TD* eagle and star border as well as *T. DANFORTH PHILAD*ᴬ marks. An examination will show that the marks are in the same place and fade off exactly the same way. In addition, every nick, scratch, cut, bump and bruise is in exactly the same position on both plates, including several dents on the rim. All of these castings are very sharp and are exactly the same. Again, a collector should be wary of multiple pieces with all these matching characteristics.

Cast Thomas Danforth III mark

Struck Thomas Danforth III mark

Note: presence of casting fault near booge is present on both plates – this defect would have been removed in the turning process on a legitimate plate

Each plate has identical scratches, pits and bumps in the same locations

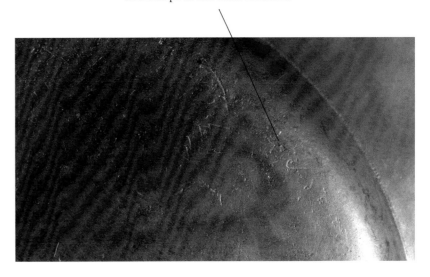

British Plate with a Fake Smith & Company Mark

This flat rim, 7¼ inch diameter plate is a well made 18th century British piece. Some parts of the plate were purposely smoothed out on the back where what appear to be British marks are barely visible. The fake mark of Smith & Company (working in the 1840s) was then struck onto the plate.

British Plate with a Fake Smith & Company Mark

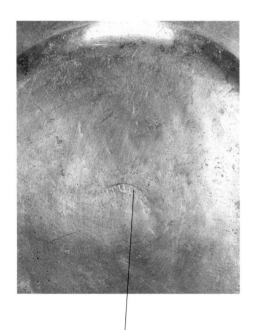

Original mark has been purposely smoothed out and is barely visible

This is a fake Smith & Company mark

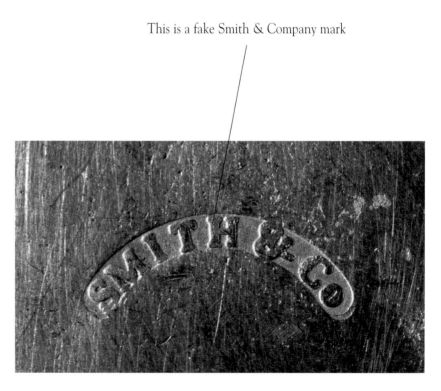

Single-Reeded Plate with a Fake Richard Lee Mark

Single-Reeded Plate with a Fake Richard Lee Mark

This is a single-reed rim plate, 8⅛ inches in diameter. At one time this plate had been silver plated, but subsequently, the silver plating was partially removed. There is considerable defacing of the front center of the plate where a mark of some kind appears to have been rubbed off.

On the back, there is the fake No. L413 mark of *RICHARD•LEE*. Here is an L413 mark again on an item which was not part of the Lees' output (see p. 73). Lee plates were a different size.

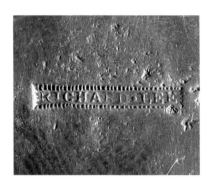

Fake Richard Lee mark

Genuine Richard Lee mark

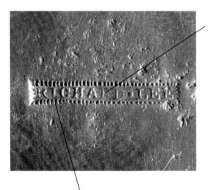

Fake mark has more distance between letters and edge

Note: fake mark has fine, evenly spaced serrations on the sawtooth edge

Letters on genuine mark are irregular and appear hand-cut

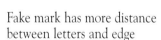

Face side of plate indicates flattening of surface and shows where original mark has purposely been rubbed off

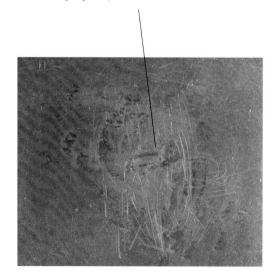

British Plate with Fake Samuel E. Hamlin Marks

British Plate with Fake Samuel E. Hamlin Marks

This is a single-reed rim British plate, 8½ inches in diameter. One can still see the British marks that appear to be those of either Thomas Swanson or Samuel Ellis.

There are also three strikes of a fake Samuel Hamlin mark. The Hamlin mark is an eagle with a banner above which includes the word *HAMLIN*, and the word *PROVIDENCE* below. The fake Hamlin marks were purposely struck at angles so that they are only partially visible. As a result, it is very difficult to accurately compare them to authentic Hamlin touchmarks.

Fake Samuel E. Hamlin mark

Genuine Samuel E. Hamlin mark

Curvature and thickness of oval is different and less refined in the fake mark

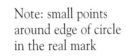

Note: small points around edge of circle in the real mark

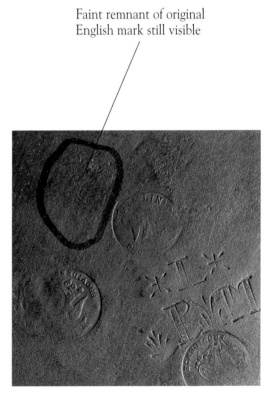

Faint remnant of original English mark still visible

Wavy-Edge Plates with Fake Marks

Wavy-Edge Plates with Fake Marks

These are a pair of five-lobed, wavy-edge plates with multiple-reeded rims. There are two marks on the back. One appears to be *VARIDO ETAIN*, with the date *1751* or *1757*, plus an animal and fleur-de-lis above the date. The second is a European-type rose and crown mark.

These are fake plates and both are identical. If the surface is examined, especially from the front, there is a little raised blip in exactly the same position on each one. These plates are cast and not lathe finished. This type of plate would never have been cast and not finished. The fake marks are not very refined and the plates have enough artificially induced patination to create the illusion of an eighteenth century plate.

These plates have been positioned to illustrate a casting flaw common to both – period plates would have been finished on a lathe

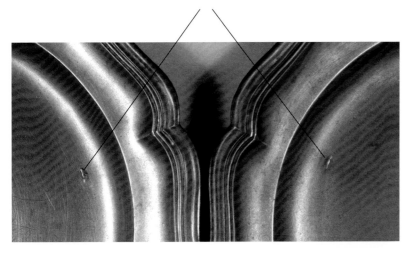

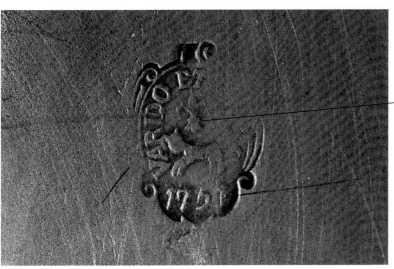

Crude marks contain just enough detail to mislead and the date could easily fool a beginning collector

Fake Continental Wavy-Edge Plate

Fake Continental Wavy-Edge Plate

This is a 9 inch, five-lobed, wavy-edge plate with a reeded edge that was cast, and a double strike of a crude rose and crown die on the back. If one looks at the edges on the back, they are unfinished, with rough areas where the edge has not been trimmed. This is a very poor example of a fake Continental plate. There is an area on the back of the plate that appears to have been filled in. One can easily surmise that, at one time, this plate had a small hanger attached to the back and was hung on the wall as a decorative piece.

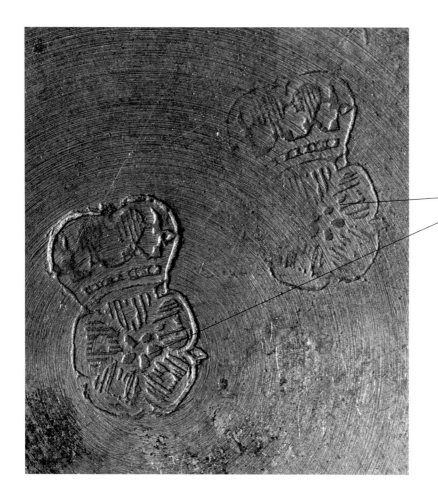

Note: fake Rose and Crown marks are flat and crude

Reproduction Plate with a Fake Frederick Bassett Mark

This is a deep concave rim 20th century plate, 9³/₁₆ inches in diameter. On the back it bears the fake *F•BASSETT NEW. YORK* mark with some distressing. A previous owner has crossed through this mark and written the word "fake." However, if this plate were a little more distressed, did not have a scratched X through the mark, and was not labeled as a "fake", it might fool some people into believing it was a legitimate Frederick Bassett plate.

Reproduction Plate with a Fake Frederick Bassett Mark

Fake Frederick Bassett mark

Genuine Frederick Bassett mark

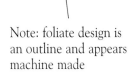

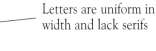
Letters are uniform in width and lack serifs

Note: foliate design is an outline and appears machine made

Letters vary in width and have serifs

Note: "hand-cut" character of die on genuine mark

J.T. Stauffer Plates with Cast Marks

J.T. Stauffer Plates with Cast Marks

These are three, single-reed, deep plates, 9⅝ inches in diameter, made by J.T. Stauffer. Two of these plates (pictured – upper left) have Nathaniel Austin eagles and hallmarks on the back. They were cast from the same mold with every pit and blemish in the same place. If observed from the front, there are obvious patterns in the pitting which are identical to one another. To put it simply, these "Nathaniel Austin" plates have been banged up and are not very attractive.

On the third plate, the Stauffer mark, *JTS* with eagle, has been struck on the back. In this case, Mr. Stauffer has taken a plate casting with Nathaniel Austin marks, scraped the marks off, smoothed it out, wire brushed the surface, and struck his own mark in the same spot. Otherwise, all three of the plates are exactly the same.

Cast Nathaniel Austin mark

Struck J.T. Stauffer mark

Cast Nathaniel Austin mark

Struck Nathaniel Austin mark

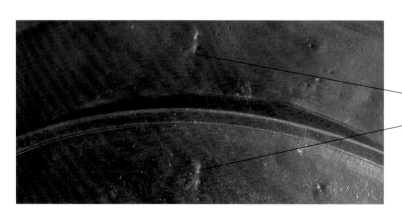

Note: casting depressions and pitting appear in the same place on all plates

Continental Dish with a Fake Thomas Badger Mark

Continental Dish with a Fake Thomas Badger Mark

This single-reed rim dish is 12³/₁₆ inches in diameter. The dish is very heavy because of a high lead content and is European in origin. It probably dates from the late 18th century or early 19th century. However, it has a fairly sophisticated fake mark of Massachusetts pewterer Thomas Badger struck quite deeply on the reverse side. All collectors need to understand that in addition to having a fake Thomas Badger mark, this piece is much too heavy to be an American dish.

Fake Thomas Badger mark

Genuine Thomas Badger mark

Note: right wing of eagle in fake mark lacks detail and both wings point straight down

Stripes in shield of fake mark are too straight and uniform in width

Eagle's right wing in genuine mark is more angular with well defined feathers

Note: letters in genuine mark are thicker and look hand-cut

British Plate with a Fake Samuel Hamlin Mark

British Plate with a Fake Samuel Hamlin Mark

This is a flat rim plate, 9 1/16 inches in diameter, and in very rough condition. Centered on the back of the plate is a straight line large *HAMLIN* mark. If one looks slightly below and above the mark, one can still see the faint, partial marks of Samuel Ellis. This is a British plate with a fake *HAMLIN* mark. There is only one example of this large, fake *HAMLIN* die. Whether another of these large *HAMLIN* marks actually exists, or whether the faker just saw a photograph of the very small *HAMLIN* mark is uncertain.

Collectors should be aware that there are numerous British plates and dishes in existence where either the mark has worn off, or it has been purposely rubbed off. Unfortunately, fake American marks have often been struck on many of these pieces.

Fake Samuel Hamlin mark   Genuine Samuel Hamlin mark

Note: fake mark does not have a serrated edge – letters on fake mark are heavy with thick serifs

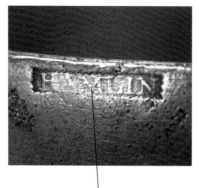

The genuine HAMLIN mark is very small and has a serrated edge – serifs on letters are thin

This repair to the rim of the plate might lead one to believe this piece is correct – repairs to a fake plate would seem unlikely

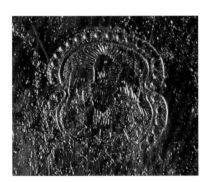

British Plate with a Fake Thomas Danforth Boardman Mark

British Plate with a Fake Thomas Danforth Boardman Mark

This is a 12⅛ inch British dish in poor condition. There are no signs of British marks because the back is so badly worn, but there are two fake Thomas Danforth Boardman eagle marks. They are the *T.D.B.* eagle with a dotted, waisted oval outline. This fake *T.D.B.* eagle mark is one of two that appear in this book (see pages 101 and 117). This mark resembles the handiwork of someone who previously made a series of fake marks including Nathaniel Austin, Samuel Danforth, and several Boardmans.

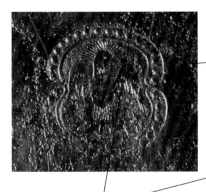

Fake Thomas Danforth
Boardman mark

Genuine Thomas Danforth
Boardman mark

While this fake mark is well executed and might fool some collectors, it lacks the depth and detail of the genuine mark

Note: curvature at the top of the fake mark is more pronounced than the genuine mark

20th Century Plates with Fake Marks

These fake marks are bulky and crude
lacking refinement and detail

20th Century Plates with Fake Marks

These are 87/16 inch, raised rim plates which resemble single-reeded rim plates. Actually the reed is raised up slightly off the surface. These plates have some very crude marks on the front. The first plate has a teapot-shaped icon within a shield and a stylized crown above. It is accompanied by a mark which has three or four stars with a bar above, and another stylized crown mark. The second plate has the same marks, but they are not as well struck.

On the reverse side of the first plate, it is obvious that this is a very poor casting. The plate appears just as it came out of the mold. There are three marks, made either from pouring apertures or from a slug that was put into the mold surface. In addition, there are some voids in the casting around the rim, with several bumps where metal adhered to the casting. This irregularity also appears on the front. The second plate has probably been sanded and then wire-brushed to get rid of all of the imperfections, but both plates are from the same mold. If one looks in the crevice where the raised reed is located around the edge, one can see all of the marks of the molded material.

These are both 20th century plates with artificial color, made of poor grade metal, with one being wire-brushed. They are not period antiques.

20th Century Saucer with Fake Marks

20th Century Saucer with Fake Marks

This is a flat rim saucer or small plate, 4 9/16 inches in diameter. It bears on the face of the rim the words, "Hampton Court" in script, leading one to believe that it may be from Hampton Court Manor House. On the opposite face of the rim are four rampant lion hallmarks in a shield-shaped device.

On the reverse of the saucer, there is a *LONDON* mark flanked by two strikes of an *X* and crown. Opposite those marks, are the initials *E.N* in a rectangle. Overall artificial aging also remains on the back. The front of the saucer has been cleaned and smoothed off.

If it weren't for the Hampton Court lettering and the other marks on it, this little saucer could be a fairly convincing antique. In reality, this item was probably made in the 20th century.

All these marks are crude and flat – the rampant lion and letters lack definition and refinement

20th Century Continental Child's Plate

20th Century Continental Child's Plate

This is a child's five-lobed, wavy-edge, toy plate, French or German in style, and about 3⅜ inches wide in diameter. It appears that someone has tried, very ineffectively, to make some hallmarks. There is the numeral 5 over a crown, which are both over an *X*. The marks look like they are machine made. In addition, this piece has been colored dramatically on the back, giving it a very dark appearance. Nitric or sulfuric acid was used to achieve this effect.

Since this was a child's piece, it may not have been made to deceive, but merely made to look old. This plate was made in the second half of the 20th century.

Note: the 5 and X marks on this plate have a modern, machine-made appearance

20th Century Oval Platters

20th Century Oval Platters

These are a pair of doll size or child size oval platters with multiple-reeded, lobed edges. They both measure 4⅝ inches on the long axis and 3¹/₁₆ inches on the short axis. Both have on the back of the platter a crown over an *X* above a *LONDON* mark.

These are 20th century items and are central European in style. In spite of the English-looking marks, this style would never have been made in Great Britain. And, the decorative marks were probably not meant to deceive anyone since these were children's toys.

Note: these oval platters have the exact same casting marks – marks that would have been removed on a period plate after finishing

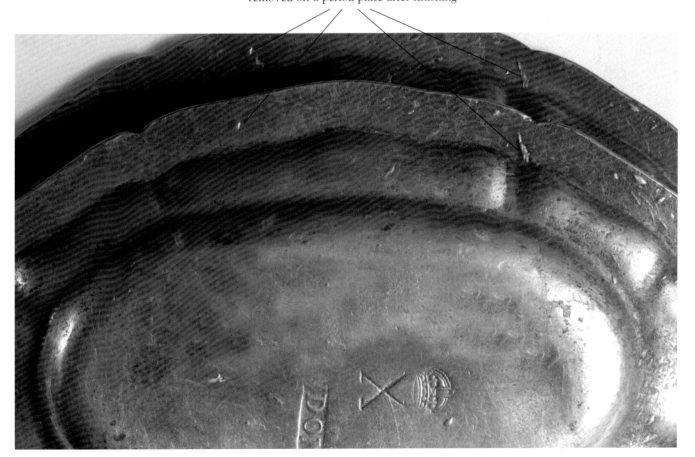

Fake Plates with Fake Touchmarks by Richard Neate

Fake Plates with Fake Touchmarks by Richard Neate

These are a pair of 7 inch, single-reed plates. The reeding is quite faint on the front of each plate to make them appear worn. The plates show false pitting, aging and buffing in order to look old. The back of both plates also indicate sporadic artificial aging with the addition of numerous scratches. These are all signs that the maker used these techniques in order to deceive.

The back of each plate has a single mark – an $S \cdot S$ over a crown with two stars below. All these icons are surrounded by an oval cartouche. Just above the oval is a crowned X touchmark. This particular mark, that of Samuel Sweetman, is a fake touchmark illustrated as #111 on page 9 of the Pewter Society's book, *The Richard Neate Touch Plate and two others of unknown origin*.

These are known fake touchmarks used by Richard Neate – they appear flat and less refined compared to period marks

Fake Decorated Continental Plate

Fake Decorated Continental Plate

This is a small, 7 15/16 inch Continental plate with a bossed bottom having a raised medallion. On the front, it has knurled decoration on the outer rim, as well as at the juncture of the rim and booge. The medallion in the center includes two birds which look somewhat like the Austrian double-headed eagle. There is also writing and engraving on the front side of the plate. The back side shows scraping, probably where a touchmark once was, and also could have been stamped, "Made in Germany". That line would have been required after 1890.

This raised medallion looks crude and may have been burned into the center of the plate

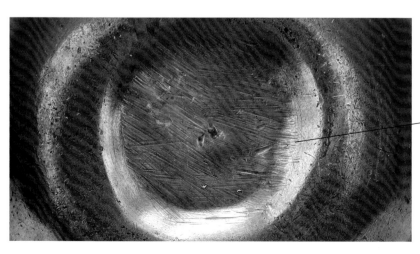

Note: the scrapings on the bottom of this plate may indicate an attempt to remove a late touchmark

Broad Rim Dish with Fake American Marks

Broad Rim Dish with Fake American Marks

This is a 14 inch broad rim dish with an engraved stag's head crest on the front. On the reverse side the following fake marks were struck: *F•BASSETT NEW. YORK* and a Boardman, no name eagle in an oval. The dish shows evidence of being cast in two or more stages. Period pieces rarely show such a process.

A period dish of this type would have dated from the 1670s. However, the maker's marks on this piece would date from the last third of the eighteenth century through the first quarter of the nineteenth century. This inconsistency is proof that this piece is a fake. Besides, the design of this broad rim dish is more in keeping with Continental pieces rather than British or American. There is a reeded support between the booge and the rim on the back of this dish. This is a feature not found on period pieces of American or British manufacture. This dish was definitely made with the intent to deceive.

Note: the eagle in the fake mark is an outline and looks mechanically made

Eagle in the genuine mark is well defined and very detailed

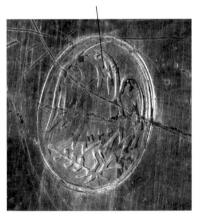

Fake Boardman Eagle mark

Genuine Boardman Eagle mark

Letters are uniform in width and lack serifs

Letters vary in width and have serifs

Fake Frederick Bassett mark

Genuine Frederick Bassett mark

20th Century Plate with Fake English Marks

20th Century Plate with Fake English Marks

This is an 8 inch, single-reed plate made of cast metal which bears the fake touchmark of William Wright, a London maker. The fake hallmarks of Ingram & Hunt (from Bewdley) are seen just below the touchmark. The hallmarks on this plate appear to be the same as on the touchplate of Richard Neate. In addition, the small, barely visible word *ENGLAND* has been inscribed on the back rim. This mark would only be found on a 20th century reproduction.

This plate is highly polished and buffed, and has no hammering on the booge. Hammering was a standard practice on almost all 18th century English flatware.

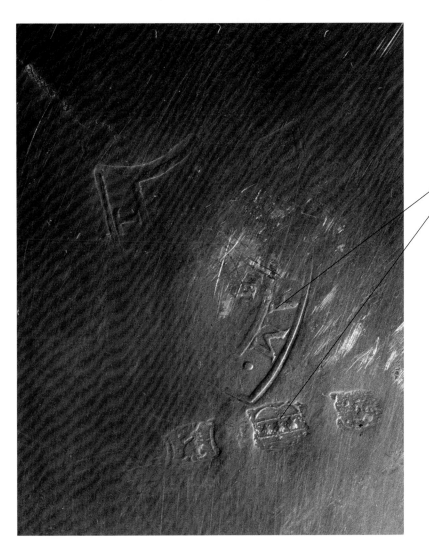

While these marks look close to the originals, they are from different manufacturers

Note: small inscribed ENGLAND mark on rim indicates this plate was made in the 20th century

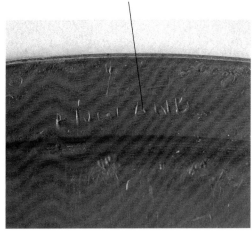

Continental Plate with a Fake Thomas Danforth Boardman Mark

Continental Plate with a Fake Thomas Danforth Boardman Mark

This is an 8¼ inch plate of Continental origin with a rim and booge design typically found on plates of the 18th and 19th centuries. Struck on the back is a fake *T.D.B.* (Thomas Danforth Boardman) waisted eagle touchmark with beaded border. The die used to strike this touchmark represents a careful attempt to create a mark that is convincing. If this was struck on a piece of American pewter in the style or design used by Mr. Boardman, it could easily fool an uninformed collector.

Please note that this fake *T.D.B.* touchmark is different from the fake *T.D.B.* mark that appears on page 164.

Fake Thomas Danforth Boardman mark	Genuine Thomas Danforth Boardman mark

While this fake mark is well executed and might fool some collectors, it lacks the depth and detail of the genuine mark

Note: curvature at the top of the fake mark is more pronounced than the genuine mark

British Plate with a Fake William Elsworth Mark

This is a single-reed rim plate, 7³/₄ inches in diameter. This plate is believed to be British, but struck on the back is an unrecorded William Elsworth mark – *WE* in a circle. This is the type of touchmark a maker would normally have used on hollowware and spoons. This fake mark is the only known example of this particular die strike. It is not a legitimate mark.

British Plate with a Fake William Elsworth Mark

Fake William Ellsworth mark

Genuine William Elsworth mark

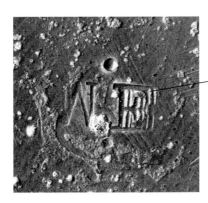

Note: this fake mark looks very mechanical and lacks the serrated oval in the genuine mark

This WE mark is believed to be the small touchmark of William Ellsworth and has been found on a few 18th century spoons

Miscellaneous

Fake Salt

This large pedestal salt has a top bowl diameter of 3⅞ inches and the diameter of the foot is 4⁵/₁₆ inches. It has good oxide, and wear and tear. Unfortunately, the pseudo hallmarks on the side of the cup are crude and are obvious fakes. The hallmarks appear to be *C.W.* (or *O.W*). In addition, there is a leopard's face and a rampant lion.

The piece has been distressed in a tumbling machine where objects were banged up against the surface. Artificial color was then induced with chemicals and artificial oxide, along with pitting, was added to the base and on the inside of the bowl.

On a period salt, one would not see this much wear on the underside of the bowl, and particularly under the foot where the surface is not exposed to abrasion.

Fake Salt

Note: the surface has been artificially aged and the pitting is too consistent to be caused by salt

Reproduction Trencher Salts

The surface of this trencher
has been artificially aged

Reproduction Trencher Salts

This pair of octagonal trencher salts was manufactured in the last quarter of the 20th century. The piece on the right has been left as it was originally made. The example to the left has been altered to make it look old.

The unaltered piece is marked. It reads "Made in Holland", and "Royal Holland Pewter", both cast in relief. The mark of Royal Holland Pewter looks like "Daalderop". It has a design in the middle with four tulips and a crown on top. It also includes the letters *K*, *M* and *D*. These letters probably represent the company that made the item. There are also the raised initials *IG* below the circular design. These are cast in relief. Aside from the fact that this piece was buffed at one time, it essentially remains as it was first produced.

The piece on the left has had the Royal Holland marks removed from the bottom. Some of the edges have been rounded, it has been distressed, and an acid treatment was applied to the entire piece. This makes it somewhat lighter and more worn in appearance.

This is a good example of how easily a piece can be altered to appear as if it was made in the 18th century.

Note: the mark has been
removed and the surface
chemically aged

This is the contemporary
touchmark of Royal
Holland Pewter

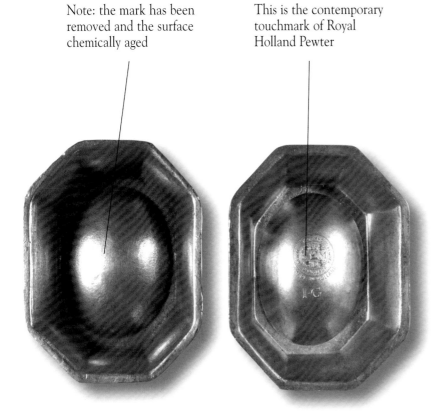

Reproduction Josiah Miller Sundial

Reproduction Josiah Miller Sundial

This is a window-style sundial 4½ inches in diameter, beautifully cast in fine metal, with the name *JOSIAH MILLER* and latitude, *42*, cast in relief. Near the center and to either side of the gnomon, are what appear to be two angel heads with wings.

The decorated side, although it is almost too smooth and too well done to be believed, is very convincing. However, with a carefully applied acid treatment it could look very much like an original Josiah Miller sundial.

The back of the sundial is very smooth unlike the surface found on period sundials. It is also marked "Stieff Pewter" and "Metropolitan Museum of Art". These markings could easily be eliminated by someone who wished to make this piece appear to be a genuine Josiah Miller sundial. If the marks were removed and the entire surface aged, it would be very difficult to tell this piece from a legitimate antique sundial.

Note: this reproduction sundial was made for the Metropolitan Museum of Art by Stieff Pewter

20th Century Sundial

20th Century Sundial

This small sundial is 3¹/₁₆ inches in diameter and is a brand new casting done by PCCA member Dr. Andrew Turano in 1993. It was made from an 18th century sundial mold in his possession.

The sundial is clearly marked on the back, *AFT 93*. This mark was stamped on after the casting. The die strike was obviously not part of the mold. Dr. Turano made no attempt to make this piece look like an 18th century antique.

While the sundial has not been artificially colored, it is remarkable that the surface casting, including the numerals and decoration, along with the gnomon, are so well done. If, however, someone did have a mold like this, or a casting from the mold, a newly made sundial could be easily "aged" to appear like an 18th century piece.

Andy Turano mark

Fake 18th Century Sundial

Fake 18th Century Sundial

Note: this WB mark is also found on fake round bowl spoons

This sundial is 9³/₈ inches in diameter. It is one of a large group of sundials which have caused a great deal of controversy over time.

This one has the word *FECIT* over a crown along with the date *1717*. There is also a fake mark with the initials *WB*.

There are several different styles of these 20th century dials. Some are square, some are round, some are made of brass and some are made of pewter. They all have certain basic similarities including style, construction and markings.
A number of these dials have the name "James Cutler and Salem" on them while others say "Salem, Massachusetts" or just "J. Cutler".

If one examines the back of this dial, one can see how the letters on the face were punched or stamped in, not cast. All of the lines and numbers have telescoped through to the back surface.

There is another fake sundial recorded made of iron, bearing the same or similar *WB* initials, and the date *1777*. It also has the letter *C* on the surface which may stand for Cutler.

These marks are crudely made to appear "primitive" and "naive" whereas most 18th and 19th century pewterers took pride in their work and applied a mark of quality

Correct British Pepper Pot with a Thomas Danforth III Mark

Correct British Pepper Pot with a Thomas Danforth III Mark

This item is generally referred to as a pepper pot or pounce pot. The height to the top of the finial is 2⅞ inches. It has a mushroom-shaped top over a cylindrical body on a low pedestal foot and bears the genuine mark of *T. DANFORTH PHILAD^A* on the outside bottom. In reality, this mark is a portion of a Thomas Danforth III plate that was cut out and soldered to the bottom of the pepper pot.

Unfortunately, this is not the way that a true pepper pot would be made or marked. In this case, the original bottom that was in the neck was cut out, then a portion of the plate was attached to the bottom of the foot. This alteration would make it impossible to clean the inside surface of the foot.

This is a case where the faker took a legitimate object and added a genuine mark to create a totally new form for an American maker.

Note: this seam indicates where the original plate was cut and then applied to the foot of the pepper pot

Reproduction Inkwell with a Fake Frederick Bassett Mark

Reproduction Inkwell with a Fake Frederick Bassett Mark

This round inkstand or inkwell is $2^{1}/_{8}$ inches high, with a base diameter of $3^{3}/_{4}$ inches. It has a lot of oxide on the upper surface and good color. The turnings on the side of the body are typical for this style of inkwell.

On the bottom is a fake Frederick Bassett touchmark. It is the *F•BASSETT NEW. YORK* mark within a fan shape. If one looks near the edge of the inkwell, one can see where the tiny word "England" has been mostly scraped off. This same style of inkwell has also been found with other makers' marks including William Will, Parks Boyd, and others.

While this is a fine looking inkwell, with the mark removed and a bit more distressing, it could very easily pass as a legitimate antique. However, this inkstand was made in the early 20th century and, because of the oxide, was made to deceive.

Fake Frederick Bassett mark

Genuine Frederick Bassett mark

Letters are uniform in width and lack serifs

Note: foliate design is an outline and appears machine made

Letters vary in width and have distinct serifs

Note: letters are "hand-cut" on genuine mark

Correct British Mustard Pot with a Fake Thomas Wildes Mark

Correct British Mustard Pot with a Fake Thomas Wildes Mark

This is a legitimate British lidded condiment or mustard pot. It is 2⅛ inches to the top of the lid with a base diameter of 2¼ inches. The lid is a flat sheet of metal with a cutout for a spoon. A small handle and thumbpiece complete the pot. Originally, this mustard pot was probably fitted with a glass liner and this piece was most likely manufactured between 1860 and 1870.

However, this mustard pot has the fake mark of Thomas Wildes (*T. WILDES*) on the inside bottom. All pieces by Wildes were marked on the outside bottom. If this mustard pot had retained its original liner, a collector could have easily missed the fake mark.

Fake Thomas Wildes mark

Genuine Thomas Wildes mark

Borders of fake mark are flat and slightly irregular

Note: letters of fake mark are thicker and wider

Borders of genuine mark are crisp

Note: letters of genuine mark are well defined

Correct Whale Oil Lamp with a Fake
Boardman & Co. Mark

Correct Whale Oil Lamp with a Fake Boardman & Co. Mark

This saucer based, cylinder font, whale oil lamp is a type that has a shaft supporting the cylinder. It is often referred to as a Boston area style lamp. It probably is in all respects a correct lamp, made by Eben Smith, James Putnam, or Morey & Ober.

However, this lamp bears the fake mark of an eagle in a circle with the words, *BOARDMAN & Cº NEW–YORK* on the inside bottom of the lamp. This is one of the many Boardman marks that have been faked over the years. As a fake mark, this one is quite well done. Were it applied to an actual unmarked Boardman item, it could be easily assumed correct.

Fake Boardman & Co. mark

Genuine Boardman & Co. mark

Downward slope of wings on fake mark is continuous, too short and lacks definition

Left wing of genuine mark is curved and bows outward

Note: border of fake mark is thin – border of genuine mark is wider

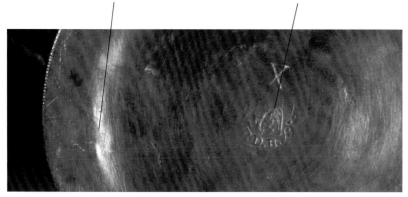

British Teapot with a Genuine T.D.B. Mark

British Teapot with a Genuine T.D.B. Mark

This drum shaped teapot with a double-domed lid bears the legitimate mark of Thomas Danforth Boardman on the outside bottom. This is the *T.D.B.* mark in a waisted oval with dots along the edge. Just above is Boardman's *X* mark.

The problem is that this pot is a British teapot, circa 1790 to 1810, with the entire bottom and part of the body replaced. If one looks inside, the crude replacement can be seen to include as much as an inch or two up the side of the body in some places, and half an inch up from the base in others. In essence, the entire lower section of this pot has been replaced with new metal.

The bottom of the teapot has been constructed from two pieces of metal. The portion with the genuine Boardman mark may have been taken from a plate. It was inserted into the center of a new piece of round metal. The fabricated bottom was then attached to the body.

Collectors should be alert to pieces with this kind of construction. In this case, the entire operation was done to deceive.

Note: the built-up area indicates where the new bottom with the touchmark was added

This is a genuine Boardman mark possibly from a plate or another piece

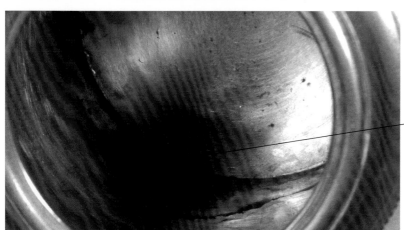

This interior section illustrates where the teapot has been fabricated and rebuilt

20th Century Wine Coaster

20th Century Wine Coaster

This wine coaster is 3½ inches across at the top and bottom, and is about ½ inch deep. On the bottom, it bears the mark *CROWN AND ROSE CAST PEWTER* and *MADE IN LONDON*. This is the mark of an English firm making pewter in the 20th century.

While this wine coaster was never made to deceive, it is a good example of a piece which, if the mark was removed or filled in, would appear to be a genuine piece of antique pewter.

Note: true 18th century touchmarks never used the words CROWN & ROSE or CAST PEWTER

The words CROWN & ROSE and CAST PEWTER are incuse: most 18th century marks have cameo (raised) letters

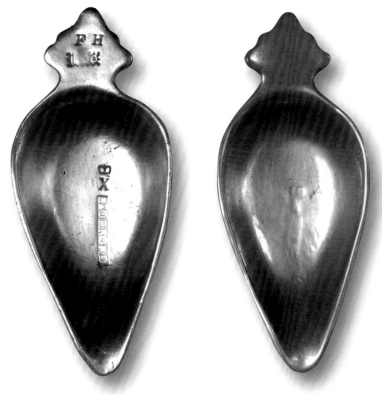

Altered 20th Century Pap Boat

Altered 20th Century Pap Boat

These items were used to feed invalids and are commonly referred to as pap boats. They both measure $4^{15}/_{16}$ inches from the tip of the feeding area to the tip of handle, with the widest point of the bowl measuring $2^{1}/_{8}$ inches. The handle is often referred to as a pine tree outline.

These items were made in a single casting and both were struck with fake marks. The pap boat to the left is clearly marked in the bowl and on the handle. The pap boat on the right, however, has had the marks almost completely buffed away. This was done to give it the appearance of a well worn antique pap boat and is a deliberate deception.

Fake pap boats have been well known in pewter circles for many years. They were apparently made to fulfill the desire of early collectors to obtain an example of a scarce form.

Note: the mark has been buffed out on purpose to disguise the age of the piece and give the appearance of wear

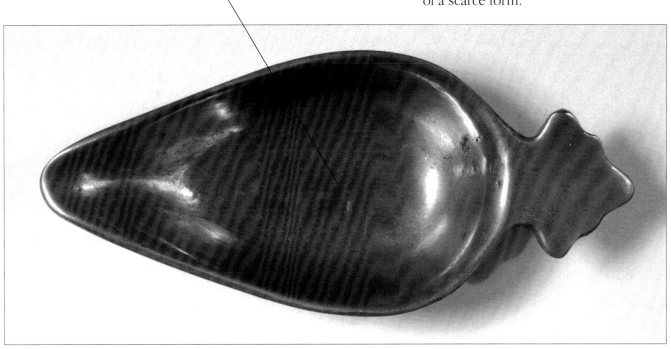

English Inkstand with a Fake Frederick Bassett Fleur-de-lis Mark

This treasury inkstand was probably made in the 19th century and is English in origin. The top of the piece measures 7³/₄ inches by 5¹/₄ inches. It has the two typical lift flaps and compartments for the inkwell and sander, both of which are missing. However, on the outside bottom is struck a fake Frederick Bassett fleur-de-lis touchmark.

Since many inkstands similar to this one were made in the 18th century, it would be easy to mistake this as a legitimate Frederick Bassett piece.

English Inkstand with a Fake Frederick Bassett
Fleur-de-lis Mark

Fake Frederick Bassett mark

Genuine Frederick Bassett mark

Note: the fleur-de-lis in the fake mark is too wide

While the fake mark is rather convincing, it lacks the beading around the border of the genuine touchmark

Note: the genuine mark includes a second, very distinctive fleur-de-lis

Fabricated Wall Sconce

This item appears to have started out as another creation of Jay Thomas Stauffer although how it ended up as a wall sconce is anyone's guess. The plate, which was most likely made by Stauffer, includes cast *SAMUEL DANFORTH* and *HARTFORD* touchmarks.

The wall sconce itself is a fabricated object and was never produced as a period piece. In this instance, a small, 19th century style handle has been soldered to the bottom edge of the plate. Then, a candle socket was applied to the handle to create the sconce. Again, the Stauffer plate alone is considered a counterfeit.

Crude solder points indicate where 19th century style handle and modern hanging wire were attached to plate

Note: Samuel Danforth mark lacks definition and was reproduced as a cast reproduction from an authentic Danforth plate

Fabricated Wall Sconce

Counterfeit English Flagon with Fake
Touchmarks by Richard Neate

Counterfeit English Flagon with Fake Touchmarks by Richard Neate

This tall English flagon is 11¼ inches from the base to the top of the finial, with a bottom diameter of 4¾ inches. It has a low double-dome lid with a two-step finial, a "ram's horn" thumbpiece and a double "C" scroll handle.

While this flagon may appear genuine, it is actually a Richard Neate product with his *NR* hallmark. Other Neate hallmarks are also included. Similar flagons by Richard Neate with fake English hallmarks also exist.

The thumbpiece, which was broken off at some point, was crudely re-soldered back on. The flagon has also been artificially aged.

One telltale sign that this piece is suspect is the swollen "entasis" or bulge to the drum. While this feature is occasionally found on early English hollowware, it is not common.

In addition, vertical parting lines from the mold on the inside are another clear indication that this piece would never have been made in the 18th century. This is not a method of construction in use during that era.

Note: the NR and rooster hallmarks are known Richard Neate symbols

Fake Johann Christoph Heyne mark

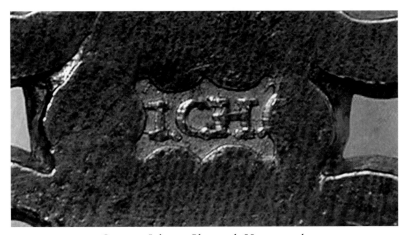

Genuine Johann Christoph Heyne mark

A Fake Johann Christoph Heyne Mark and a Fake TD&SB Mark

To the left, we see both fake and genuine marks of Johann Christoph Heyne and Thomas D. Boardman and Sherman Boardman. Both of these fake marks are relatively well done. The quality of the letters in the fakes closely resemble the style used in the legitimate touchmarks (see other false *TD&SB* marks on pages 71, 74, 78, 111, and 112). Fortunately, in both cases these fake marks were found on objects which were not produced by Heyne or the Boardmans. Had they been struck on an unmarked piece appropriate for either maker, a collector might not give these marks a second thought.

The images displayed on this page reinforce the necessity of photo comparisons using genuine touchmarks when considering a piece for purchase.

Fake Thomas Danforth Boardman & Sherman Boardman mark

Genuine Thomas Danforth Boardman & Sherman Boardman mark

Summary

The authors and editors of this book hope that this study has added to the reader's knowledge and understanding of antique pewter. We understand that there is always more a student of this subject can learn. The reference books cited in the Bibliography of this volume are excellent sources of information.

For additional information about antique pewter, visit the Pewter Collectors' Club of America (PCCA) Web site at:

http://members.aol.com/pewterpcca

This site covers many aspects of pewter and pewter collecting. It also has information on membership and the two semi-annual club publications: *The Bulletin* and the *PCCA Newsletter*.

In addition, the club holds national and regional group meetings where various topics on antique pewter are discussed.

We urge readers to consider membership in the organization.

Glossary of
Terms

Glossary of Terms

This glossary contains terms that apply to American pewter and to British pewter that was imported into this country from the late 17th century to the first quarter of the 19th century. For terms that apply only to British pewter, refer to the Web Page of The Pewter Society and follow their link for a glossary of British pewter terms.

Acid Treatment   A method of cleaning pewter with acid. Also a process utilizing acid on pewter to give it an aged appearance.

Alloy   A mixture of two or more primary metals created in order to alter physical properties available with only a single primary metal.

Antimony   A metallic element used in pewter alloys as a hardening and brightening agent.

Anti-Wobble Ring   A raised ring on the bottom of a lid which fits inside the opening of a container in order to keep the lid from moving laterally.

Baluster   An adjective used to describe a hollowware form with a slightly bulbous body; usually associated with measures.

Basin   A narrow rim deep bowl, most often used domestically.

Beading   A narrow decorative molding resembling a row of small beads formed by a beading tool, in somewhat the same manner as a pie crimper, applied with pressure against the edge of a rotating pewter piece in a lathe.

Beaker   A cylindrical drinking vessel used for domestic and ecclesiastical purposes, usually with a molded base, a larger diameter at the top than at the bottom, and often having a pronounced flair to the upper lip.

Bismuth   A metallic element used occasionally in pewter alloys as a hardening agent. Bismuth expands while solidifying which allows more alloy to expand into the mold cavity.

Boardman   Refers to Thomas Danforth Boardman, his brothers Sherman and Timothy, and the various partnerships formed by the Boardmans during the first half of the 19th century. Beginning in 1804 and ending in 1873, this Hartford, Connecticut based family created the largest and longest-running pewter making business in the early history of the United States.

Bobeche   A rounded cup inserted into a candlestick to catch drippings and to aid in the removal of the candle stub.

Booge   The curved side wall of a plate or dish between the bottom and brim.

Brim   The broad, flattened upper edge or rim of a plate or dish surrounding the deeper body of the piece.

Britannia   An English trade description for a hard lead-free pewter alloy developed in England in the 18th century, made more durable and lustrous than the previously used alloy by the addition of a higher percentage of Antimony.

Burned On   A metal-to-metal fusing process. See Linen Mark.

Camphene   A volatile, turpentine-derived liquid fuel used for lighting.

Casting	Process whereby molten pewter is poured into a mold to form the desired article. This was the main way of forming pewter articles until the introduction of Britannia metal allowed articles to be cold-formed from sheet metal. However, even then casting continued to be used for certain articles such as measures. It was also used to form the knops, handles, feet etc. of articles whose bodies were made from sheet metal.
Caster	A pierced-top container used to dispense salt, sugar or sand.
Caster holder	A frame, usually mounted on a broad base, which holds small bottles of salt, pepper, oil, vinegar, mustard, etc.
Chalice	A stemmed cup used for both domestic and ecclesiastical purposes.
Charger	A term for large dishes – not usually applied to American flatware but commonly used in England. See Flatware.
Chatter marks	Coarse radial marks extending outward from the center, usually on the bottom of plates, dishes, porringers, mugs, etc., caused by a vibration of the skimming tool used on a lathe while finishing off a rough casting.
Corrosion	The slow formation of a dark layer on the surface of pewter over time. Depending on the alloy, the corrosion can range from a very thin and hard layer to a thick and crusty scale. This differs from the "graying" of bright pewter with time which can be easily removed by polishing.
Crenate	A decorative scalloped edge, as on some tankard lids.
Dam	See Linen Mark.
Dies	Engraved hard metal punches used to impress a mark (or touch) in pewter for the purpose of identifying the maker, the quality, or the owner of that piece.
Dish	See Flatware.
Dome lid	A rounded lid type found on flagons or tankards.
Double-dome lid	Another type of flagon or tankard lid with a stepped dome that gives the appearance of a smaller dome atop a larger one.
English export pewter	English pewter exported to America from the late 17th century through the first half of the 19th century. Several forms such as pear-shaped teapots and creamers, drum-shaped teapots, and sugar bowls were made specifically for the American market and are rarely found in England. At the time of the American Revolution as well as today, there are more pieces of English export pewter to be found in the United States than pieces made by American pewterers.
Eruption	Oxidation (corrosion) of the pewter which has resulted in surface bubbles.
Fake	A piece made purposely to deceive prospective buyers.
Ferrule	Socket on pewter teapots, coffeepots, etc. into which wooden handles are inserted, pinned, and thus attached.

Fillet
A narrow, slightly raised band often used around the body of a hollow-ware piece for decoration and/or to strengthen a construction joint.

Finial
A small, cast ornament topping the lid or cover on a teapot, flagon, sugar bowl, etc.

Flagon
A lidded serving container for liquid, typically used ecclesiastically to carry wine for the sacraments. Used domestically as well.

Flashing
Excess pewter found around the edges of a new casting caused by molten metal flowing out from a seam in the mold. Flashing is cut off and discarded during the finishing process.

Flat lid
As opposed to dome lid. Describes an American tankard lid type made in the 18th century but patterned on the English flat lid tankards (Stuart tankards) of the 17th century.

Flatware
Name given to pewter such as plates and dishes, to distinguish it from hollowware. A more modern term for sadware.

Flatware Nomenclature (Diameter – American vs. English)

Name	American	English
Saucers	N.A.	5" to 7"
Plates	5" to 10"	7 1/2" to 10"
Dishes	10" & larger	10" to 18"
Chargers	N.A.	18" & larger

Saucers were not made in American pewter and were out of fashion in England by 1700. Small American plates in the 5 inch to 6 inch range are called butter plates and marked ones are rare. The largest known American dish is 19 inches; the largest known English charger is nearly 36 inches.

Flux
A substance such as glycerin and acid used to clean two pieces of metal to be joined together with solder. Flux also aids the flow of solder over the joint.

Font
In pewter lamps, the closed reservoir which holds the liquid fuel (whale oil, camphene, etc.).

Garnish
A set of flatware for the table, traditionally a dozen of each size.

Gill
A unit of volume equal to a quarter of a pint.

Gimbal lamp
A lamp attached to its base by a double axis suspension device which allows it to swing freely and remain upright when the base is moved in any direction.

Gnomon
The triangular column or pin on a sundial that casts a shadow to indicate the time of day.

Hallmarks
Similar in appearance (but not meaning) to hallmarks used by gold and silversmiths. Designed by the maker and presumably used to make pewter appear as much like silver as possible.

Hollowware	Pieces made to hold liquids such as mugs, tankards, teapots, pitchers, flagons, measures, etc., as distinct from flatware.
Incuse vs. Cameo	To leave a dimensional impression using a hammer versus a profile cut in raised relief.
Journeyman	A trained craftsman working for a master pewterer.
Knop	A bulge or knob on the stem of a chalice, candlestick, or lamp for decoration and convenience in holding.
Knurled	A series of small beads pressed or cut into a metal edge. When used in a decorative mode, it consists of lines (straight or curved) in a band – sometimes found around the lid, body or base of hollowware and sometimes found around the edge of flatware.
Lathe	A machine upon which work is rotated around a horizontal axis and shaped, skimmed, or cut by a fixed or hand-held tool.
Linen mark	The handles of porringers and some other pewter vessels were attached by fusing the metal without solder. A handle mold with openings at points of connection was placed against the finished body of the vessel and then filled with molten pewter, which melted part of the body at the joint, forming a strong bond. A "tinker's dam", a heat-absorbing bag of linen or other coarse material filled with dry sand, was pushed against the inside of the vessel during the procedure. This usually left an imprint of the cloth – a "linen mark" – in the softened metal behind the exterior application of the handle mold.
Maker's mark	A touchmark which was struck on his wares by a pewterer in order to identify him as the maker of the article.
Mark	See hallmarks, maker's mark, secondary mark, touchmark and verification mark.
Married piece	An item made up of components not originally intended to be together.
Measure	A commercial container of standard capacity regulated by government inspectors who periodically verified the capacity and placed verification marks on the container.
Mug	A lidless, handled container of various forms and standard capacities usually used to hold beverages such as beer, ale, or spirits. Mugs are usually larger in diameter at the bottom than at the top.
Multi-reed	A descriptive term for a plate or dish with several decorative reeds or moldings at the outer edge of the brim, usually cast, but occasionally incised.
Oxidation	One of the processes which contributes to the corrosion of pewter over time.
Patination	The surface appearance of any object caused by age and use; a patina.
PCCA	Pewter Collectors' Club of America.

Pewter
An alloy consisting predominantly of tin, but alloyed with other metal(s) to make it stronger and harder. Metals that have been alloyed with tin include copper, antimony, bismuth and lead.

Plate
See Flatware.

Planish
To give a smooth finish to metal by repeated striking with a smooth faced hammer. A technique used by 17th and 18th century English pewterers and 18th century American pewterers to give a more finished appearance to intricately designed porringer handles. It is especially noticeable on "Crown Handle" designs but was used on other designs as well. The practice was discontinued in the 19th century.

Porringer
A small bowl with usually one flat handle cast onto the side of the bowl. Pennsylvania "Tab Handle" porringers, however, have a plain handle cast as an integral part of the bowl. Most porringers have decorative and intricately cast handle designs. The basic handle types are: Crown; Old English; Flowered; Hearts & Crescent; and Solid or Tab.

Provenance
Attributions of maker, owner, or geographical origin.

Quaich
A Scottish term used to describe a shallow drinking vessal with two handles, usually made of wood or metal.

Rat-tail
A tapering extension or thickening of a spoon handle onto the underside of the bowl as either a support or decorative element.

Reed
The molding, usually cast, around the edge of flatware; multiple or single denoting the style of the period in which it was made.

Repousse
Relief decoration formed by hammering from the underside.

Reproduction
A piece made to appear as an older form with no intention to deceive the buyer as to age.

Ringed foot
A metal ring applied to the base of an item (usually hollowware) which elevates the bottom from a flat surface. Rings were applied to objects in order to reduce wear, protect the underlying surface, and as a decorative element.

Sadware
See Flatware.

Scale
Hard oxide on pewter. Severe deterioration of pewter prone to flaking with rough handling.

Scrape marks
Visible tool marks that remain after manually removing surplus metal and smoothing rough surfaces of cast pewter. Spoons and mug handles often show such marks.

Seaming
A forming technique used in the manufacture of Britannia cylindrical vessels where a sheet of pewter would be bent into the desired shape, the joint where the ends meet bonded with solder, and the resulting seam disguised through polishing and placement under an attached handle. Usually more visible on the inside of a vessel.

Secondary marks
Any mark other than an identifying touchmark which was struck on his/her wares by a pewterer. Common secondary marks include hall-marks, a crowned X mark, city or location marks, and owner's initials.

Single-reed	A descriptive term for a plate, or dish with a single cast reed or molding at the outer edge of the brim (on the upper surface). Popular from the 18th century into the 19th century.
Skimming	The process of removing surplus metal and smoothing rough surfaces of cast pewter by scraping with a tool as the piece rotates on a lathe.
Skimming marks	Indentations left by skimming tools, usually found on the backs of plates, the outside bottom of porringer bowls, basins, mugs, tankards, and areas less frequently seen and therefore not as carefully finished.
Slush cast	The casting method used in pewter manufacturing to create hollow appendages such as handles and spouts. Hot pewter poured into a cool mold solidifies around the contact with the mold, allowing the still molten core to be poured out.
Solder	An alloy, usually of lead and tin, which melts relatively easily and is used to join pieces of metal such as pewter. As a verb, the process of joining metals with a solder bond.
Spinning	Process of forming an article by mounting a piece of sheet metal on a chuck and forcing it over a form while it is rotating, usually on a lathe.
Spline	A metal strip or shaft sometimes found on the back of porringer handles to add strength.
Stamping	Process of forming an article by stamping a piece of sheet metal over a form in a press.
Sweat solder	The process of applying heat to solder in order to join two pieces of metal together.
Tankard	A cylindrical drinking vessel with a handle, a hinged cover, and a projecting thumbpiece for raising the cover or lid. Tankards are usually wider in diameter at the bottom than at the top. Unlidded drinking vessels are usually called "mugs".
Touchmark	See Maker's mark.
Verification marks	Government inspector's marks placed on a commercial vessel certifying that the vessel was of proper standard to dispense a specific volume or measured amount, e.g. pint. Pieces may have been initially verified at source of manufacture, but were certainly verified periodically at their place of use as well. American verification marks are usually found only on baluster measures made in America or imported from England.
Waisted oval	A term used to describe an oval shaped pewter mark with pinched-in sides whereby the ends are wider than the middle.
Wavy edge	A piece of flatware whose rim is formed of curved segments.
Wrigglework	Zigzag type of engraving in pewter, made by walking a screwdriver-like tool from corner to corner of the blade to form the desired design.

Bibliography

The following list of books on pewter was chosen by the Pewter Collectors' Club of America for their relevance to the topics discussed in this volume.

1. Cotterell, Howard Herschel. *Old Pewter, Its Makers and Marks in England, Scotland and Ireland: An Account of the Old Pewterer and His Craft.* Second edition, Rutland, Vt.: Charles E. Tuttle Company, 1963. (First edition, London: B.T. Batsford Ltd., 1929).

    This book is a must for any collector of British pewter to identify the pewterer, his mark or marks, dates and places of his work. The marks are drawn (rather than photographed) so this is one small limitation. There is an index of "devices" used in a mark to help one to identify the maker. Finally there are large illustrations of both the London and Edinburgh Touchplates.

2. Davis, John D. *Pewter at Colonial Williamsburg.* Williamsburg, Va.: The Colonial Williamsburg Foundation (in association with University Press of New England), 2003.

    This book illustrates the finest collection of British pewter in the U.S. with a few outstanding American pieces. The primary focus is on eating and drinking vessels.

3. Dubbe, B. *Tin en Tinnegieters in Nederland.* Ontwerp: De Tijstroom Lochem BV, 1978.

    This is the standard reference book on Dutch pewter. For an English speaking scholar the book's primary values are: excellent photographs, detailed drawings of all known Dutch marks, and English summaries of all thirteen chapters.

4. Ebert, Catherine. *Collecting American Pewter.* New York: Charles Scribner's Sons, 1973.

    This writing provides historical data, explains how pewter pieces are constructed, but does not assume American pewter was as faked as British pewter. The author distinguishes old pewter from reproductions based on "feel".

5. Fennimore, Donald L. *American Pewter/British Pewter, The Charles V. Swain Collection.* Doylestown, Pa.: privately published by Masthof Press, Morgantown, Pa., 2002.

    This catalogue highlights one of the premier private collections of American and English export pewter in the U.S. and includes past articles by the collector from the Pewter Collectors' Club of America (PCCA) semi-annual publication, *The Bulletin*.

6. Gadd, Jan. *Pewter Candlesticks: English Candlesticks of the Second Half of the 17th Century.* Welshpool, U.K.: The Pewter Society, 2004.

    In addition to the excellent photographs and descriptions of pewter candlesticks in this book, there is also an important chapter on fakes. This particular chapter, while focusing on fake marks and the fake construction of candlesticks, has valuable information as to how and why pewter fakes appeared during the 20th century in England.

7. Hall, David. *Irish Pewter, A History.* Welshpool, U.K.: The Pewter Society, 1995.

    In addition to the history of Irish pewter with illustrations, this book contains helpful Irish verification and capacity marks. There is a complete list of 506 Irish pewterers, most of their touchmarks, and a brief glossary of pewter terms.

8. Hall, David. *Types of Irish Pewter.* Welshpool, U.K.: the author and the National Museum of Ireland, 2005.

This book continues the study of Irish pewter with good illustrations. It has an important section on Haystack measures (often faked) with a five point test for the authenticity of this form. Further research on Irish pewter is shown in a very extensive bibliography.

9. Herr, Donald M. *Pewter in Pennsylvania German Churches.* Birdsboro, Pa.: The Pennsylvania German Society, 1995.

This book contains specific information on the use of pewter in these churches with good details on church pewter decoration and excellent photography. It also contains descriptions of the pewterers whose work is still represented in these churches today.

10. Hornsby, Peter R.G. *Pewter of the Western World 1600-1850.* Exton, Pa.: Schiffer Publishing Ltd., 1983.

In addition to a brief history of the Pewter Industry, the numerous illustrations are good examples of decorated pewter. The chapter on marks has brief information on Continental, British and American pewter. The majority of the contents are photographs of various forms of pewter.

11. Jacobs, Carl. *Guide to American Pewter.* New York: The McBride Co. Inc., 1957.

This is practical listing of American pewterers, their pewter with drawings of their marks and a 1957 price list of the pewter. At the end of the book, there are drawings of known porringer handles and various teapot shapes.

12. Kauffman, Henry J. *The American Pewterer, His Techniques and His Products.* Camden, N.J.: Thomas Nelson Inc., 1970.

Kauffman gives detailed descriptions of a variety of pewter pieces and how they were made, with both construction designs and illustrations of the finished product.

13. Kerfoot, J.B. *American Pewter.* New York: Bonanza Books, 1924. 500 Illustrations.

This writing is the earliest definitive description of American pewter forms. After discussing the metal and what to collect, it then outlines the history of pewter before and after 1750. The value of this book is in the photographs of the marks, not just drawings. Much of this information in this volume has been updated in more recent publications.

14. Laughlin, Ledlie Irwin. *Pewter in America: Its Makers and Their Marks.* Second edition, Vols. I and II. Barre, Mass.: Barre Publishers, 1969.

This is the most authoritative book on American pewter. It includes information on each American pewterer by region. It also describes the how and why of faking pewter, how to clean pewter as well as what to do and not do in collecting.

15. Laughlin, Ledlie Irwin. *Pewter in America: Its Makers and Their Marks.* Vol. III. Barre, Mass.: Barre Publishers, 1971.

This volume updates all information on this subject which has been found since the original publication of Vols. I & II in 1940. Of particular value is the checklist of all American makers of pewter, britannia or block tin and an extensive, 22-page bibliography.

16. Montgomery, Charles F. *A History of American Pewter.* New York: A Winterthur Book, Praeger Publishers, 1973.

    Montgomery describes various forms of pewter in eight chapters with an entire chapter devoted to connoisseurship. He has illustrations of 18th century pewterers which help to put the pewter within an appropriate historical framework. There are photographs of the various marks of American pewter.

17. Osburn, Burl Neff & Wilbur, Gordon Owen. *Pewter: Spun, Wrought, and Cast.* Scranton, Pa.: International Testbook Co., 1947.

    These authors go into great detail on all aspects of constructing a pewter object with detailed drawings, diagrams and measurements.

18. Peal, Christopher. *Pewter of Great Britain: for pleasure and investment.* London: John Gifford, 1983.

    This reference is an excellent, authoritative history of pewter in Britain from 350 A.D. to 1900 A.D. Peal includes chapters on collecting, cleaning and repairing as well as identifying fakes and reproductions.

19. Pewter Society. *The Richard Neate Touch Plate and two others of unknown origin.* United Kingdom: The Pewter Society, 1996.

    This is the first publication devoted entirely to exposing known fakes in the U.K. It illustrates photographs of marks on the Richard Neate touchplate alongside the authentic mark from the London touchplate. There is a brief note on Neate – The Man written by John Richardson. This small book does not profess to have the last word on fakes as The Pewter Society is aware of Continental reproductions and forgeries.

20. Sterner, Gabriele. *Pewter Through Five Hundred Years.* Christie's South Kensington Collectors' Guides. London: Studio Vista, Cassell Ltd., 1979.

    In addition to its historic and stylistic information, it also gives valuable tips on identifying fakes. There is an excellent glossary of pewter terms to help the novice collector.

21. Thomas, John Carl. *Connecticut Pewter and Pewterers.* Hartford, Ct.: The Connecticut Historical Society, 1976.

    All pewter and pewterers who came out of Connecticut are described, illustrated and listed. Their marks, genealogy and some sales catalogs are also shown.

22. Thomas, John Carl. ed. *American and British Pewter, An Historical Survey.* New York: Main Street/ Universe Books (The Magazine Antiques Library), n.d.

    This book is an excellent compilation of articles on pewter reproduced from *The Magazine Antiques.* These short informative articles are divided into three categories: British Pewter, American Pewter before 1800, and American Pewter after 1800. Charles Montgomery and Percy Raymond discuss the English influence on American Pewter, and Eric de Jonge discusses the Swedish influence on American Pewter.

23. Wolf, Melvyn D., M.D. *An American Pewter Collection, The Collection of Dr. Melvyn & Bette Wolf.* Salt Lake City, Ut. Family Heritage Publishers, 2006.

   This catalogue illustrates the most comprehensive collection of American pewter ever assembled. An excellent reference tool on American pewter forms, what makes this catalogue especially useful are the numerous informative comments which accompany many of the pieces.

24. Wylie, W. Gill. *Pewter: Measure for Measure.* n.p., 1952.

   Wylie describes and illustrates the variety of English, Scotch, Irish, American and French measures with a table showing the dates and specific forms produced in each national region.

Index

Index

Index

Notes

Notes

Notes